PETER HANDKE AND THE POSTMODERN TRANSFORMATION

JEROME KLINKOWITZ AND
JAMES KNOWLTON

PETER HANDKE AND THE POSTMODERN TRANSFORMATION

THE GOALIE'S JOURNEY HOME

A LITERARY FRONTIERS EDITION
UNIVERSITY OF MISSOURI PRESS
COLUMBIA, 1983

FOR OUR DAUGHTERS, NINA AND LARA

University of Missouri Press, Columbia, Missouri 65211
Library of Congress Catalog Card Number 83–6867
Printed and bound in the United States of America

Library of Congress Cataloging in Publication Data

Klinkowitz, Jerome.
Peter Handke and the postmodern transformation.

(Literary frontiers)
Bibliography: p.
1. Handke, Peter—Criticism and interpretation.
I. Knowlton, James, 1943– . II. Title.
III. Series.
PT2668.A5Z75 1983 838'.91409 83–6867
ISBN 0–8262–0420–1

PREFACE

Few figures in contemporary writing are as strikingly innovative as the Austrian poet, playwright, and novelist, Peter Handke, who was born 6 December 1942, at Griffen in the southern province of Carinthia. At the close of an era dominated by such elder spokesmen as Thomas Mann and Hermann Hesse, he seized international fame at the age of twenty-three. In all genres his literary works defied both long tradition and current topicality of interest by displaying the brash style of a self-conscious aesthetic radical, from his transcription of the Japanese hit parade as poetry, through his hurling of insults at the audience as drama, to his rehearsal of the semiotic process as fiction. Though an heir to the Austrian fascination with language that has produced the most rarified artistic and philosophical treatises, his achievements have eclipsed the avant-garde experimentalism of the Vienna Group's H. C. Artmann and Germany's Helmut Heissenbüttel to become widely popular and genuinely accessible work.

Yet it is the world against which Handke reacts that gives his work such a remarkably high profile and allows us to integrate it within the larger rejection of modernist axioms known as *postmodernism*. The simplest formulation of how the postmodern aesthetic transforms literature was made as early as 1929 by Samuel Beckett, who in "Dante . . . Bruno. Vico . . Joyce" set a seemingly impossible standard for *Finnegans Wake,* at the time Joyce's work-in-progress: "His writing is not *about* something; *it is that something itself.*" The modernist sensibility, however, grounded as it was in the certainties of psychology and myth, continued to resist this challenge, insisting literature should be something that represents and interprets the world; such was the lingering state of affairs Peter Handke faced with his initial performances and publications. For German-language fiction of the postwar decades, socially committed realism was not only a popularly accepted form but was also a style reinforced by discussions among the most prominent authors who had been brought together for annual meetings as Group 47. Throughout the 1950s, theater remained classical in disposition thanks to heavy state subsidies, which in turn glamorized the form and drew audiences increasingly wealthy and conservative. In the tradition of Goethe's Weimar, poetry had become highly respectable as well—to the point at which Handke could object that it no longer did the work of the imagination, but instead pandered to preconceived expectations for art. The social disruptions in West Germany during the 1960s, notably absent from Handke's politically tame Austria, served to politicize literature and further enhance its referential qualities, with a Marxist theory propounded by Marcuse, Bloch, Adorno, Horkheimer, and later by Habermas becoming the most influential critical approach.

In the mid-1960s, when Peter Handke burst upon the scene with his attacks upon both audiences and established writers alike, the times were ripe for literary rather than simply political revolution. How he has grown from this initially radical stance into a writer who maturely articulates the postmodern aesthetic in German today is the subject and structure of our book, which traces the embattled goalie's anxiety for the imaginative death of literature to his successful journey home as a leading proponent of the New Sensibility transforming German and Austrian culture.

Our greatest debts are to the University of Northern Iowa, with its Summer Institute at Klagenfurt, Austria, and to the Camden College of Arts & Sciences of Rutgers University, which have supported our work; to Professors Jan Robbins and Fritz König for professional aid and encouragement; to Professors Manfred Pütz (Bamberg) and Marc Chénetier (Paris and Orléans) for Handke materials; to Stephen Dixon, Richard Kostelanetz, and Michael Stephens for corrective readings, and to Julie Huffman-Klinkowitz for editorial help. All students of Handke are indebted to Nicholas Hern and June Schlueter, whose respective studies of his early drama and translated works have made our own investigations of Handke's postmodern theory and of his many as yet untranslated novels, stories, and recent play much easier to undertake. Where translations exist, we have cited the American first editions; otherwise, parenthetical page references are to the original German or Austrian volumes listed in our bibliography, with the exception of *Begrüssung des Aufsichstrats (Greeting the Board of Directors),* which is more widely available in the Suhrkamp anthology of Handke's early works, *Prosa Gedichte Theaterstücke Hörspiel Aufsätze* (1969).

Jerome Klinkowitz
Cedar Falls, Iowa

James Knowlton
Klagenfurt, Austria

1982–1983

CONTENTS

I. Peter Handke and the Postmodern Aesthetic

> These boards don't signify a world. They are part of the world. These boards exist for us to stand on. This world is no different from yours. You are no longer kibitzers. You are the subject matter. The focus is on you. You are in the crossfire of our words.
>
> —*Offending the Audience*

Literature is a way of looking at the world, and thanks to his emphatically postmodern habits of perception, Peter Handke has emerged as a leader in the transformation of the modern sensibility. In one of his earliest essays, Handke described what he learned about his own way of dealing with outside existence. Looking out the window one day, he observed two foreign workers sweeping the street below. "Both were wearing orange and white striped jackets *like bicycle racers*," he noted, italicizing the terms of similarity, and "both wore baggy, wrinkled pants *like bums or characters in a Beckett play.*" Nor did the comparisons stop there: "Both had faces *like Southern Europeans.* Both were wearing hats *like POWs from the First World War.* Both walked with stiff knees and flat feet *like drunks.*" Soon Handke found that his perceptions were quite spontaneously running amok through encyclopedic references to art as well as life, for "With their gigantic brooms and shovels they looked *like figures in a painting by Breughel.*"[1] But what of the workers themselves? Handke had to admit that his compulsion to look elsewhere for points of reference prevented him from seeing the street sweepers as anything other than a system of displacements. Casting out his net to catch reality, Handke drew back with his object unsnared.

1. Peter Handke, "*Theater und Film*: Das Elend des Verleichens" ("*Theatre and Film*: The Misery of Comparison"), *Prosa Gedichte Theaterstücke Hörspiel Aufsätze* (Frankfurt: Suhrkamp, 1969), p. 314.

And yet a strange thing had happened: once this process took over as an automatic activity, reality became the net itself.

How, Handke asks, do we come to this compulsion to compare, to perceive things only in relation to other things? Isn't it simply because of our linguistic inability to express details as verifiable in themselves—to negotiate that unbridgeable distance between the name for a thing and the thing itself? And why is it, he continues, that when we compare we always want to evaluate? Given that hopeless gap, the linguistic materials we have to work with (which the theorists conveniently call *signifiers)* exist only so that we can play them off each other, measuring their relative distances as a substitute for embracing the objects in themselves. French philosopher Jacques Derrida agrees that in language we have no absolute identities, only a system of differences, and Peter Handke's genius has been to devise a way of writing poems, plays, and novels that capitalize on this linguistic condition. By comparing, Handke argues, we never pretend to be dealing with the actually existing objects, the *signifieds*—rightly so, because our language provides no means of absolute identification. Instead, we create a hierarchy in our consciousness within which each new perception finds its niche. Consciousness selects terms for comparison as if it were a customer evaluating wares on the shelf, for such are the linguistic signs by which we transact our business with the world and with each other. Consequently, we never leave the supermarket of signs, just as in language we never escape the system. We never see things themselves, only relations.

What distinguishes postmodernism in general and Peter Handke's work in particular is not simply the recognition of these linguistic and philosophical terms, which date back to Ferdinand de Saussure's *Cours de linguistique générale* (1916) and Ludwig Wittgenstein's work with the Vienna Circle in the decades between the two world wars, but the positive advantages for literature these conditions are seen to provide. Far from regretting this utter distinction between the signifying word and the signified object that caused the modernist sensibility to seek refuge in irony or to plumb the depths of mythology and the psychological for some essential grounding of human affairs, postmodernism celebrates the rupture between language and event as an occasion for true imaginative freedom. With no determining center of authority, human discourse is free to create itself without threat of totalitarian control; no single view of reality can be legitimately imposed, for reality itself is no longer an externally verifiable standard but becomes just an arbitrary system composed democratically among the linguistic relationships agreed to by the speakers. What modernists such as T. S. Eliot and Thomas Mann mourned as the death of the book (as a meaningful anchor of reference), the postmodernists would celebrate as the birth of writing: the quintessentially human act of play with only provisionally referential materials.

Handke's arguments for a new literature have been paralleled by equally revolutionary calls for a new literary theory. In 1966 he made his international debut by challenging the unexamined realism of Germany's most prestigious writers, assembled at Princeton University for a conference on "The Writer in the Affluent Society." In the same year, Jacques Derrida, as a similarly emergent European upstart, presented his ideas about self-apparent linguistic signs to Johns Hopkins University's International Colloquium on Critical Languages and the Sciences of Man, one of the key events from which developed the new theory of deconstruction as an alternative to the dogmatically structuralist thought that had characterized modernism in decline. Derrida's position outlines the transformative sense of the linguistic and philosophical rupture that shows its effect in such literary work as Peter Handke's:

> Henceforth, it was necessary to begin thinking that there was no center, that the center could not be thought in the form of a present-being, that the center had no natural site, that it was not a fixed locus but a function, a sort of nonlocus in which an infinite number of sign-substitutions came into play. This was the moment when language invaded the universal problematic, the moment when, in the absence of

> a center or origin, everything became discourse—provided we can agree on this word—that is to say, a system in which the central signified, the original or transcendental signified, is never absolutely present outside a system of differences. The absence of the transcendental signified extends the domain and the play of signification infinitely.[2]

In this infinite play of signification may be found the roots of Handke's radically optimistic attitude toward the elements of rational dissolution, which drove so many classic modernists to despair. "Things fall apart," William Butler Yeats is famous for lamenting: "The center cannot hold." Yeats's own conclusion, announced in the title of his poem "The Second Coming" (1920), was that "mere anarchy is loosed upon the world" and would rage beyond control until a transcendental order was restored. Handke's distance from this typically modernist quest for meaning—whether mythic, psychological, or as in Yeats's case religious—becomes evident when we consider what a positive approach to the infinite play of signification implies. Far from viewing signification as anarchistic and in need of externally imposed reform, postmodernism seizes the opportunity to recast literary works with a new sense of pertinence for human activity. Rather than fret about the moral impossibility of connecting with reality, Handke prefers to locate literature within the process of constructing fully provisional meanings. And in so doing, his poetry, drama, and fiction are reinvented for our new philosophical times.

Ihab Hassan has described a set of contrastive phenomena that shows how a shift of emphasis from the signified object to the play of signifiers changes the face of literature.[3] Where the moderns sought purpose, the post-

2. Jacques Derrida, "La structure, le signe et le jeu dans le discourse des sciences humaines," collected in *L'écriture et la différence* (Paris: Seuil, 1967) and translated by Alan Bass as "Structure, Sign, and Play in the Discourse of the Human Sciences, " *Writing and Difference* (Chicago: University of Chicago Press, 1978), p. 280.

3. Ihab Hassan, "Postface 1982: Toward a Concept of Postmodernism," *The Dismemberment of Orpheus: Toward a Postmodern Literature*, 2d ed. (Madison: University of Wisconsin Press, 1982), pp. 267–68.

moderns celebrate play; hierarchal principles of order yield to nonpredictability, as less emphasis is placed upon the finished work than on the process of creation. Instead of totalizing a sense of existence, the postmoderns deconstruct it, revealing how fraudulent any reductive summations must be, based as they are on principles we now recognize as mere assumptions. Metaphor, employing as it does a transcendental sense of illusion with one entity asked to become another, is replaced by metonomy, in which the process of having a part stand for the whole lets each constituent element retain its own identity. An eagerness for depth is replaced by a fascination with surface: texts are therefore "writerly" rather than "readerly," for there is no compulsion to find meaning beyond the author's performance on the page, which the reader is invited to re-create. Yet the product is not meaningless, because writing can be celebrated for the human activity it really is, rather than for its futile attempt to represent something else. Determinacy and transcendence, the twin goals of modernism that directed final purpose away from the artwork itself, lose favor with postmodern writers, whose new respect for the materials of their art encourages a sense of immanence within the text at hand. Above all, the author's obligation to signify what is real reliably and to be judged by the accuracy of that signification is no longer argued, urged, or regretted when the process necessarily fails. Instead, as a self-conscious system of differences rather than identities, language can be appreciated as an appealing dance of man-made signifiers whose highest form is not the correspondence with an ideal of order but rather a display of the artist's compositional sense of how the game of life is played.

It takes but little imagination to see how Peter Handke was born into a political and literary heritage that embodied the living absence of Derrida's transcendental signified. The Austro-Hungarian Empire of Handke's ancestors, ruled for a remarkable sixty-eight years by a single figure (the Emperor Franz Josef, modern history's classic image of benevolently paternal authority) and dominating European politics for more than a century, in 1918 completely vanished from the map, providing an object lesson in just how provisional the assumed standards of reality were. The First Austrian Republic that followed soon fell victim to political bickering so divisive that civil war and enforced union with Nazi Germany were in some quarters welcomed as relief from chronic instability. The Nazi experience, however, only served to discredit received notions of authority all the more, until the postwar Second Republic took refuge in neutrality and an accommodative coalition government that absolved politics of any potentially abrasive function and thereby of meaningful debate. In Handke's Austria even literary life was decentralized: the Holocaust had effectively destroyed Vienna's avant-garde and created a vacuum to be filled by cautious celebrants of the postwar status quo, leaving literary innovations to the provincial centers of Graz and Salzburg where the issues of modernism bore no canonical authority. Peter Handke, born amid the dislocations of wartime and—after an isolated, rural upbringing—sent to the University of Graz just as the 1960s began, was suitably positioned to become the postmodernist literary man.

Handke's background spans the German-language experience of recent decades, as the national and cultural identities of Germany and Austria suffered through the central political and historical convulsions of the modern and then the postmodern ages. His birthplace, Griffen, is a rural village in the partly Slovenian province of Carinthia—a lingering trace of the once grand synthesis of languages and cultures known as Austria-Hungary, now rescattered into many of its original elements. Was young Peter a Slovene or a German? An Austrian or a citizen of the Third Reich? Such questions, which had been settled in other parts of Europe much earlier in the century, were still to be decided in the virtual tabula rasa of simple Griffen. In his memoir of his mother's life and death, *A Sorrow Beyond Dreams* (1972, translated 1975), Handke recalls that even following the First World War, "The general indigence was such that few peasants owned their land. For practical purposes, the conditions were the same as before 1848; serfdom had been abolished in a merely formal sense" (p. 7). Hence, the Anschluss and sudden entry into the war brought a fresh sense of currency to this sleepy, rural backwater. "We were kind of excited," Handke recalls his mother telling him. "For the first time, people did things together. Even the daily grind took on a festive mood." Handke characterizes the years just before his birth through his mother's "newly attained awareness of being alive":

> For once, everything that was strange and incomprehensible in the world took on meaning and became part of a larger context; even disagreeable, mechanical work was festive and meaningful. Your automatic movements took on an athletic quality, because you saw innumerable others making the same movements. A new life, in which you felt protected, yet free. (p. 14)

Yet this sense of meaning was short-lived, as the war effort collapsed and his mother's life became once more anonymous and meaningless; she ended it in suicide thirty years later, in the same village where she and her son were born.

Six December 1942: military historians will note that Handke's birthdate falls during the siege of Stalingrad, the first of many German reversals that again changed the face of central Europe. Handke himself was the natural son of an already married bank clerk working as an army paymaster, the one love of his mother's life. For convenience, she wed a German sergeant stationed in Austria, who moved the family to his native Berlin until the bombing drove them back to rural Griffen. From 1944 through 1948 they lived once more in the devastated capital, in what after the surrender became the Russian sector; escaping to Austria is one of Handke's earlier childhood memories. First destined for the priesthood, then for law, Handke addressed most of his energies as a student at the University of Graz (1961–1965) to writing. Here he was befriended by the cultural group Forum Stadtpark: a sometimes raucous and nearly always iconoclastic assemblage of poets, dramatists, fictionists, artists, and intellectuals who had just the year before pressured the city of Graz into letting them take over an old cafe in the municipal park. Alfred Kolleritsch's *Manuskripte* became the literary organ of this "Graz Group," and in its pages Handke's short stories, beginning in 1963, first appeared. The new writer's breakthrough came in 1966, as his novel *The Hornets* was published to largely favorable reviews by the large and intellectually prestigious firm of Suhrkamp in West Germany, his play *Offending the Audience* became the hit of the "Experimenta I" drama festival at Frankfurt's Theater am Turm, and his proposals for a revolutionary aesthetic had their first international forum at the Princeton meeting of Group 47, where Peter Handke was the youngest and, as it turned out, the most effectively vocal writer in attendance.

The rapid transition from the provincial avant-garde of the Graz Group to prominence among the discussions of Group 47 helps to show how Handke has evolved his work self-consciously within and against the German tradition of meetings and movements. Günter Grass has celebrated this spirit of common-minded debate in his fictionalization of the devastated conditions of 1647 following the Thirty Years War. *The Meeting at Telgte* (1979, translated 1981) is Grass's allegory for an actual meeting convened three centuries later by Hans Werner Richter as Germany began to clear the rubble of an even more disastrous world conflict. The association of writers formed at this meeting, named for its year of founding, became a major force in postwar literature, coming to include Günter Grass himself, Heinrich Böll, Peter Weiss, and many other luminaries. The group's origins can be traced to a newsletter, *Der Ruf,* published by prisoners of war interned in the United States, which was continued in the American Occupation Zone during 1946 and 1947 by Richter and Alfred Andersch. In his history of Group 47, Siegfried Mandel summarizes the political roots of its approach to a postwar German literature: "the freedom and unity of Germany, a social-humanistic foundation for the new political structure of Germany, a unified socialist Europe, no imposition of the idea of collective guilt upon the German people, and no unnecessary humiliation of

Germans."[4] That Germany, West and East, failed to develop this way did not deter the mainstream German-language writers from using their novels and plays as vehicles for commentary on the country's political past and social future, as works like *The Tin Drum* (Grass), *Absent Without Leave* (Böll), *The Deputy* (Rolf Hochhuth), and *The Shadow of the Body of the Coachman* (Weiss) attest. Even in this last work, the traditional German taxonomies of social class and manners remain the author's true subject—an aesthetic position Handke found both obsolete and abhorrent.

At Princeton, Handke accused the literature of postwar Germany of having betrayed its commitment to form and of slipping back into an authoritarian moralism of content such as the members of Group 47 had themselves condemned two decades before when the memory of politically controlled literature had been fresh. To this young man for whom the great experimental dramatists such as Samuel Beckett and Bertolt Brecht were historically distant figures, for whom the currently celebrated novelists Günter Grass and Heinrich Böll were as liable for ridicule as any aging symbols of authority, and whose own work rode the crest of the first wave of postmodernism in a way that the early innovations of compositional self-reflection and paginal integrity could become conventions as discardable as the fat to be skimmed from chicken soup, Group 47 was moribund in both its theory and its practice of literature. To confuse fiction with sociology, poetry with moralized instruction, and drama with the same actions one might encounter in the office or at home was to ignore the distinctions postmodern thought had made so critical. "People fail to recognize that literature is made with language and not with the things that are described with language," Handke objected, and hence their critical measures are all askew. Once correspondence to reality becomes the standard, "the words for the objects are taken for the objects themselves," utter heresy in the face of postmodern language theory. But worst of all, to continue with such illicit identifications

4. Siegfried Mandel, *Group 47: The Reflected Intellect* (Carbondale: Southern Illinois University Press, 1973), p. 3.

would be to deprive writing of its remaining purpose: "One ponders over the objects which one calls 'reality,' but not the words, which are in fact the reality of literature."[5] To continue writing realism in a postrealistic age, Handke regretted, would be to deprive literature of any valid reason for existence.

In a work of fiction or poetry, the reality is not what is signified but the materials of sign making themselves, just as in a play, "Every word, every utterance onstage is dramaturgy . . . my words are not descriptions, only quotations . . . the only possibility they point to is the one that happens while the words are spoken on the stage."[6] This is how Handke transformed his own style of writing and what he claimed was missing in the older, more established literature of the age. No empty formalism or escapist plea of art for art's sake, Handke's essays and interviews of succeeding years continued to argue for the necessary readjustment of literature in an age that demanded real things and not discredited representations: "What bothers me is people's alienation from their own speech. In a way, this is the basic trouble with the young revolutionaries in Germany: they're alienated from their language. It isn't *their* language anymore, so they can't even communicate. The way they speak shows how wretchedly ensnarled they are in themselves."[7] For language to have any effect, it must address its own reality: not the terms of hierarchal value in a political movement that hoped to be antiauthoritarian and not the suspension of disbelief that by definition robbed literature of its meaning. Was such a shift from signified to signifier a difficult act? Not at all, Handke explained, recalling his success with *Offending the Audience:* "All you have to do is turn to the spectators and start off; with a perfectly simple shift of ninety degrees you have a new play, a new drama-

5. Quoted by June Schlueter, *The Plays and Novels of Peter Handke* (Pittsburgh: University of Pittsburgh Press, 1981), p. 5. A good news report on the meeting is provided by J. P. Bauke, "Group 47 at Princeton," *New York Times Book Review,* 15 May 1965, pp. 43–45.

6. Artur Joseph, "Nauseated by Language: From an Interview with Peter Handke," *The Drama Review* 15 (Fall 1970): 57.

7. Ibid., p. 61.

turgy." And the audience will welcome the change because of the renewed sense of seeing something *real.* "Now they suddenly felt that the theatre spoke directly to them and that this was what they had been missing."[8] The rectangular relationship in all literature—in which characters converse, narrators describe, or poets reflect while viewers and readers simply observe—was unnecessary. Rather than passively attend to the representation of another reality, audiences would be far happier having their own realities involved. If these secondhand illusions were dropped, Handke says, content would not necessarily disappear: "It would already exist in the audience . . . it would be their world. . . . I didn't omit anything, I merely abstracted."[9] He thereby gives both the artwork and its audience their own strongest justification for existence. In this way, "The theatre is not then portraying the world," where Brechtían calls to action can be dismissed as playful entertainments; rather, "The world is found to be a copy of the theatre."[10]

Literature that socializes or politicizes robs both reform and art of their integrity—such was Handke's explanation for the weakened status of each. He regretted that Group 47's allegiance to an outdated and discredited realism flew in the face of an entire generation's progress, from the Vienna Group of Gerhard Rühm, H. C. Artmann, and Konrad Bayer in the 1950s to Handke's own Graz Group emerging ten years later—both of which were extending the irrealistic aspects of literary writing. Whereas the Vienna Group's literary experiments with concrete poetry and language-play took place in the rarified air of specialists performing for specialists, however, the Graz Group, with a neither literary nor ideological program, flourished as a loose association of eager young writers whose literature addressed a wider audience and who frequently drew attention to themselves by their antiestablishment antics so

8. Ibid., p. 58.

9. Jack Zipes, "Contrary Positions: An Interview with Peter Handke," *Performance* 1 (September–October 1972): 64.

10. Peter Handke, "Brecht, Play, Theatre, Agitation," *Theatre Quarterly* 1 (October–December 1971): 90 (translated by Nicholas Hern).

natural to the brash, countercultural exuberance of the 1960s. And in this distinction lie the roots of Peter Handke's success at applying the postmodern aesthetic to everyday concerns. The Vienna and Graz groups share a fundamental skepticism regarding language as a social institution. But whereas Artmann's dadaistic banalization of the familiar and Rühm's penchant for anarchy led to a self-imposed alienation (celebrated in fiction by Bayer's grotesque anti-situations and Oswald Wiener's narrative stasis), Handke's radical critique of language has employed more familiar forms. Each group, for example, had placed near the top of its list of priorities an attack on Austrian provincialism, but instead of being consumed by this antibourgeois attitude (which produced the *antiheimat* tradition no less restricting than the style of country novel that it mercilessly satirized), Handke's innovations have struck to the heart of the matter of literary and linguistic integrity—a strong and constructive approach, aiming at a more fundamental critique of social man.

Hence, when Handke titles his most famous essay "I Am an Ivory Tower Dweller," the reference is self-consciously ironic, for his argument here and elsewhere is that for writers to keep in touch with the world they must not simply reflect but rather add their own self-apparent creations to it. "A form of representation, the first time it is applied to reality, can be realistic," Handke admits in this essay. Upon even an initial recurrence, however, "It is already a mannerism, is unreal, even though it may again characterize itself as realistic."[11] Taking for granted Beckett's dictum that literature should not be about something but rather *be* something itself, building on Wittgenstein's belief that to understand a sentence is to understand language, and adding the caution that in acquiring only a delusive mastery of language one is mastered oneself, Peter Handke set about writing in full awareness of our times. If his narrators were to describe, it would be with a system of signs; if his characters were to struggle in life, it would be

11. *Prosa*, p. 264 (as translated by Schlueter, *Plays and Novels of Peter Handke*, p. 12).

with life's semiotic process. In these ways literature could be most personally real; what you see, Handke has insisted, is what you get. His novels, poems, and plays would not depend upon socially clichéd attitudes to trigger responses in his readers, reminding them of what they had been told before. Instead, his writing would exist at the level of sign-making itself, and all action would take place within this linguistic drama of its signifying process, which readers and viewers could practice as readily as the author himself and with an equal sense of participating in an actual event.

"Narratives and novels really have no story," Handke told June Schlueter in 1979. "What is 'story' or 'fiction' is really always only the point of intersection between individual daily events." In recent works, therefore, Handke has adopted the mode of what he calls "the epic," in which "there is no expansion of character or plot, but an 'I' is writing a narrative poem about the time in which he lives, about the self, and about others."[12] Handke's most recent work can be described as a journey home to his personal concerns, a development that has contributed to the New Sensibility[13] characteristic of the newest German writing. This movement doest not reject social activism but emphasizes instead an immanent, subjective critique of the overwhelming power of the factual residing in our social institutions, the labyrinthine complexity of which seems impenetrable to literary discourse. To counteract this power, Handke focuses his attention on the individual as subject. His critique discards sociological and historical categories in favor of epistemological and phenomenological ones, emphasizing production itself rather than the finished product. He creates in his recent works a new phenomenology of the "I" as a perceiving and knowing subject immersed in a threatening world. By this Cartesian process, the writer establishes the singularity and intersubjectivity of

12. Schlueter, *Plays and Novels of Peter Handke*, pp. 172–73.

13. This wide-ranging English-language term was introduced into German cultural discussions during the later 1970s and comprises both the "new inwardness" (*neue Innerlichkeit*) of peace-movement politics and the "new subjectivity" (*neue Subjektivität*) of literature.

his own consciousness and then proceeds to reexperience the world, object by object. Handke's three prose works and minimally theatrical play of the late 1970s and early 1980s provide us with a protocol of consciousness reexperiencing and recreating the outerworld, thus reconstituting it as innerworld with a new concreteness and coherence.

Handke's first novel to express this change fully is *Slow Journey Home* (1979), in which the protagonist, a geologist working in a remote Indian village of Alaska, painfully reconstructs through contemplative vision and self-conscious sketching the surface structure of his surrounding landscape. The result is objective knowledge permeated with subjectivity, with geology functioning as a topos of Handke's new Cartesian phenomenology: the rediscovered "I" discerns, classifies, and describes the perceived world and thus secures it as personal knowledge with an intersubjective component. All four of Handke's recent works share this epistemological skepticism; at the same time, they demonstrate the author's searching for new forms of self-constructed myths with which individually perceived reality might be tied into a new system of signification validated by its maker's sense of personal control.

Peter Handke, once the young rebel, has in this latest stage of his career assumed the status of an established spokesman for what have become mainstream postmodern concerns. After the self-conscious aesthetic radicalism of his early work, he has settled into a mature style that creates valid human dramas out of the materials of language; what was once a revolutionary statement may now be accepted, without argument or passion, as the simple given conditions within which art functions. Handke's drama and poetry parallel this development, but fiction remains his favorite genre. Indeed, it is the most accessible part of Handke's canon and provides a true index to the absorption of postmodern ideas into popularly accessible art.

II. An Apprenticeship in Fiction

> I expressed approval in places where the expression of approval was prohibited. I expressed disapproval at times when the expression of disapproval was not desired. I expressed disapproval and approval in places and at times when the expression of disapproval and the expression of approval were intolerable. I failed to express approval at times when the expression of approval was called for. I expressed approval during a difficult trapeze act in the circus. I expressed approval inopportunely.
>
> —*Self-Accusation*

Peter Handke is one of those rare individuals who achieved international fame as a novelist without having his first books of fiction widely translated. Yet his novels *The Hornets* (1966) and *The Peddler* (1967) and his stories collected as *Greeting the Board of Directors* (1967) were instrumental in launching his German-language reputation and even today provide helpful examples of the methods he developed to counteract the death-of-the-novel arguments so prevalent during the social and intellectual turmoil of these years. With the stability of chronological time, irreducible psyches, and concretely realistic things all in debate, certain theorists claimed that the novel had lost its claim to legitimacy. Those who wrote on in the old mimetic way were behaving, as Susan Sontag objected, more like "journalists or gentlemen sociologists and psychologists . . . writing the literary equivalent of program music."[1] Anaïs Nin, whose own innovations in fiction lacked a sympathetic readership for twenty years, was more adamant about the great loss for art. "It is a curious anomaly that we listen to jazz, we look at modern paintings, we live in houses of modern design, we travel in jet planes," she noted in 1968, "yet we continue to

1. Susan Sontag, *Against Interpretation* (New York: Farrar, Straus and Giroux, 1966), p. 11.

read novels written in a tempo and style which is not of our time and not related to any of these influences." Although Peter Handke's successful reinvention of the novel would not be known to American readers until the early 1970s, a study of his early fiction shows that his efforts were part of the first wave of innovative fiction that from Europe to North and South America would eventually fulfill Nin's prescription for a "new swift novel" that "could match our modern life in speed, rhythms, condensation, abstraction, miniaturization, X rays of our secrets" as "a subjective gauge of external events . . . born of Freud, Einstein, jazz, and science."[2]

The postmodern transformation of fiction in which Handke's work takes part has been a long time coming—due partly to our emotional attachments to the meaning-centered standards of literary modernism, but principally to the attractively (if deceptively) mimetic promises of unexamined language itself. As both Nin and Sontag indicate, the history of art in our century has been, for the most part, the progressive disappearance of represented action in the work itself—whether painting, music, drama, or poetry. The magnitude of this revolution is such that it overturns many of art's central assumptions, from moral argument and meaning to the very existence of content. This disruption of aesthetic tradition has been most challenging to fiction because the building blocks of a writer's art—unlike daubs of paint or notes of music—cannot easily escape the implications of habitually conceptual reference. Since writing has taken this radical turn only within the past two decades and because novels and stories are the artworks closest to the concerns of daily life, the full force of this literary disruption has come to signify the special character of our postmodern experience.

How does one justify such drastic change, which for fiction means the loss of recognizable settings, of measurable plots and instructive morals, and of characters so real they might walk off the page and into the familiar concerns of our lives? Why should the novelist abandon the hard-

2. Anaïs Nin, *The Novel of the Future* (New York: Macmillan, 1968), p. 29.

won privilege of representing the values of the middle class, which over the two centuries of the novel's rise had formed the Great Tradition—equal in effect to the classical mode wherein the gods taught, heroes enacted, and poets strove to record? Why, in other words, should literature succumb to that seemingly inhumane abstractionism that produced action painting in art, nonpredictability in music, and apparent chaos for the arts in general?

Why? Because in the past three-quarters of a century our Western world view has changed, perhaps as dramatically as with the philosophical readjustments that signaled the ends of the Middle Ages and the Renaissance. Science offers the first clue, which a writer as astute as the young Peter Handke could note in popular behavior as well. *In our times, all systems—even those on which we rely for our most fundamental principles of belief and action—have become suspect.* In other words, the postmodern world with all its challenges to absolutes had become the pure writer's playground, for the arbiters of scientific thought had concluded that *all systems are fictions.* By showing how the very presence of an observer interferes with what might otherwise happen, for example, physicist Werner Heisenberg refuted the Newtonian notion that an experiment can be measured. This is the famous Uncertainty Principle, which when marshalled with the equally revolutionary hypotheses of relativity, indeterminacy, and complementarity makes for a fundamental change in how scientists view reality. Philosophy and its technological stepchildren have undergone the same disquieting revolution, culminating in a style of information theory: indicating that the maximum amount of information, the prize possession of the nineteenth-century thinkers who would isolate the thing in itself, produces only what systems analysts call "noise"—absolutely no meaning whatsoever. As for language, its basis as a system of differences determines that the object itself, fiction's previously assumed "content," is never really there, because all the narrator can provide is a set of comparisons and contrasts. Systems for commerce and belief are systems only; absolutely verifiable content is nil.

Yet life goes on, and the most sensitive among us—the creatively imaginative artist—becomes even more important as culture develops. Artists by definition tend to foreground the system of their work, and it is the building of systems that has now become the most important of human activities, replacing the shibboleths of content that by their imperiously static nature deserve the epithet *inhumane.* As Harold Rosenberg said of abstract expressionist painting, in a formulation easily transferred to literature, the artwork is no longer merely a surface on which to represent but rather "an arena in which to act."[3] What goes onto the page is not a description of an event but an event in itself. The process becomes its own reality and by that fact can be valued.

By virtue of its constructive sense of imaginative play, Handke's writing has allied itself with the positive rebuilding of postmodern fiction in the 1960s. Rather than stripping perceived objects of anthropomorphic projections so that the world might exist in absolutely neutral clarity, as the French *nouveau roman* of Alain Robbe-Grillet and Nathalie Sarraute did in the 1950s, Peter Handke's fiction has shared the playfully creative sense of Gabriel García Márquez's magic realism, in which truth is regarded skeptically, as just one version of reality, one that can be challenged by the momentary persuasiveness of a rival narrative account. In Britain, the fabulations of John Fowles and John Berger have celebrated the manner of storytelling beyond the substance of content, just as serious American fiction in the decade after the deaths of Hemingway and Faulkner produced a new breed of writer interested less in establishing dominant sexual or historical identities than in unleashing narrative time and space, as the innovations of Kurt Vonnegut, Donald Barthelme, and Ishmael Reed have shown. What all of these fictions emergent in the 1960s have in common is not just a distrust of conventional narrative realism but an exuberant delight in subverting old assumptions.

Into this atmosphere of impending change Handke intro-

3. Harold Rosenberg, *The Tradition of the New* (New York: Horizon, 1959), p. 25.

duced his first fictions: *The Hornets,* disconcertingly dense; *The Peddler,* playfully obtuse; and a collection of stories, *Greeting the Board of Directors,* which attacked or self-consciously abandoned most conventions of traditional narrative. In Handke's work, character would no longer be coherent; nor would be plot, action, theme, or any of the traditional expectations readers might bring to a work of fiction. All to be counted on were words—and Handke used them with a flourish. As the young writer formally protested at Group 47's Princeton meeting, Wittgenstein had taught that all problems in the world are preeminently matters of language, so here was where the novelist's interest should be. The proper study of mankind was no longer man, these early works demonstrate, but language as system. And what better place to see language at work as a self-consciously creative system than in fiction?

Like Márquez's *One Hundred Years of Solitude,* Fowles's *French Lieutenant's Woman,* Vonnegut's *Slaughterhouse-Five,* and Barthelme's *Snow White,* Handke's *Hornets* is written in a way to frustrate realistic readings. The novel's size (some 280 pages, long by Handke's standards) and its extraordinary complexity provide for the meaning-centered reader an unpleasant struggle through a morass of confused and confusing perceptions, images, and prose constructions. A description on the Suhrkamp edition's dust jacket offers an accurate introduction to the novel and to some of the problems involved in reading it:

> *The Hornets* is an attempt to describe the origin of a novel. A man read a book years ago; or he didn't even read the book; but rather heard about it from another source. But now, on one particular day in one particular summer, he is reminded of the long forgotten book—by a similarity in something that happens to him and to the blind protagonist of the novel—a novel he only thinks he has read years ago.

The vagueness of this description—bordering, in fact, on deception—corresponds closely to the haziness of the novel's own narration. The fragments of plot, the varying narrative perspective, and the unclearly defined characters yield no solid plot structure. Like the French *nouveau roman*, Handke's novel neglects the conventions of retellable plot, well-rounded characters, and omniscient narration—all of which suggest that things may be connected independently of perception and its processes. In his first novel, Handke thus rejects the suppositions of realistic storytelling. But unlike the French experimentalists, he is not concerned with tangible things as such, which their strict phenomenology of method is designed to reveal, but rather with "things" made only of words. Writers have presumed an identity of word and object; thus, Handke indicates, they have believed that by manipulating words they control reality. Language has been wrongly taken as a glass through which we view the world of objects, a premise now dismissed by theorists as utterly wrong. In *The Hornets*, Handke merely describes linguistic surfaces and contours, allowing the world of objects to appear only as language itself encodes it: strange and yet sharply focused, lacking the apperceptional dimension and filtering through consciousness that we traditionally expect of reality mediated by fiction.

Handke's narrator, one of four children, grows up in a rural area of Austria, presumably during and shortly after World War II. Otherwise, time in the novel has no clear dimensions. The narrator is blind, but his recollection of a novel once read indicates that his blindness is a later development. Yet even here lies a constant doubt as to the truth of his perceptions, because his narration is an inextricably intertwined mixture of his own perceptions, past and present, and his memory of the novel. The reader never knows whether he is reading about the novel's recapitulation or the narrator's direct experiences, for language alone can make no such distinction. In other places the narrator quotes directly from the reports of others, including his brother and sister. These reports are often presented in the subjunctive, usually as a second-person narrative. The narrator is also subject to a breakdown of experience, in which he is unable to distinguish between the subjective and objective components of perception. He tells of a dream in which "what I saw was no longer outside of me. . . . Also no spatial difference separated me from [what I saw], and no distance of the kind that can be measured by a yardstick could be overcome by going from the place where I was to the place where that which I was seeing was" (p. 220). The narrator's sense of spatial estrangement is further emphasized by a strangeness of things:

> Something told of something: another thing, that was not something, listened. I, who was not something, listened to that which listened and was not something, and, in spite of that, wasn't aware of it. In the rooms there had been chairs and benches, beds and tables. In the sink a bubble had burst. All of that . . . made me feel astonished and amazed, and I became greatly bewildered and had no names for anything in the house. But I perceived it. (p. 98)

Later, the narrator conjures up series of images until he reaches, as he says, "the outer limits of experience" (p. 92), at which point he loses altogether the ability to perceive in word-pictures: "Again and again I repeated the names of these sounds and gave the names of the sounds the names of the images and the names of the images the names of the sounds . . . but I couldn't create an image of any of these" (p. 93). The narrator experiences total estrangement from the outerworld and can no longer use images as symbols for distinct and defined experience. What remains is pure and unmediated experience: "I didn't see what I saw through the eye, but rather through the flickering of inanimate objects themselves, which I no longer felt as something different and separate from myself" (p. 220).

As in Handke's later Paris journal, *The Weight of the World* (1977), the narrator of *The Hornets* avoids all selection and weighting of one perception over the other; all things are accorded an equal value. The narrator's relation to reality is disturbed, as reflected not only in his failure to distinguish things in themselves but also in his inability to distinguish the sources of his experience—whether reports, a once-read novel, or direct perception of ongoing events. His approach to reality requires multiple mediations, which still do not yield clearly defined knowledge. The reality of the book in the narrator's memory and his direct experience are constantly and unconsciously mixed and blended so that a new—and ambiguous—reality arises. Fragmented fictions and memories reveal a world full of change and devoid of static being: the world as possibility.

The Hornets is therefore not a novel about reality per se; rather, it is about the medium in which the real manifests itself and in which the reality of the innerworld, to use a term preferred by Handke, confronts the outerworld: the medium of language. In *The Hornets,* Handke attempts to estrange language, this medium through which all perception, experience, and knowledge must otherwise flow, thus creating for the reader a sense of insecurity. Yet the motive is positive: to expand the reader's consciousness by challenging its structure as the apperceptional apparatus that orders and defines experience to make knowledge. In the process, readers learn not only how novels are made but how their own dispositions create reality in a supremely active way. The systematics of language here becomes an aid rather than an obstacle to writing fiction.

In 1967 Handke published his second novel, *The Peddler* (contracted but not yet translated into English), an odd little book of about 120 pages, which is modeled on the formulas of the mystery story. It follows all the rules of that familiar genre, yet it is anything but a mystery in the traditional sense, just as *The Hornets* deconstructs itself as a novel. A creature of the postmodern aesthetic, *The Peddler* devalues content so that the system-making form behind it all can become more obvious—and more enjoyable for itself.

The novel's protagonist, a nameless and faceless peddler, discovers a murder and quickly becomes the prime suspect himself. He is arrested, questioned, and beaten. He escapes, only to discover another murder. But what is its nature? Who is the murderer? We get no answers, for the novel has no plot, no defined characters, and most emphatically no solutions. Even the peddler is not sure what is happening, nor does the reader ever find out who committed the murder and how. Instead of working with specific detail, offering clues and evidence to the reader, Handke presents disjointed abstractions. A typical sentence in this novel is the model of an ideal situation, not an actually transpiring one. All the persons, materials, situations, and props for a mystery are present, but the novel's narrative structure makes no connection between them. *The Peddler* is not *a* mystery story: it is *the* mystery story—a synthesis of all possible mysteries.

In an essay written in 1967 and collected in *Prosa Gedichte Theaterstücke Hörspiel Aufsätze,* "I Am an Ivory Tower Dweller," Handke commented on *The Peddler*, then a work-in-progress:

> For the novel on which I have been working I took as vehicle the model of a fiction. I didn't invent a story, I found one. I found an external plot sequence which was already complete: the plot structure of the mystery novel, with its clichés of representation such as murder, death, terror, fear, arrest, prosecution, torture. In thinking about these I recognized modes of behavior, forms of existence, habits of experience of my own. I recognized that these automatisms of representation had their origin in reality, that they had once been a realistic method. Thus if I could make myself conscious of the models of death, terror, pain, etc., then I could, with the help of these *reflected* models, show real terror, real pain. (pp. 271–72)

Thus, Handke did not *invent* a story, he *found* one: the mystery as subgenre. Handke's novel is therefore an abstraction rather than a recreation of reality: he has extracted the essence of the mystery story and used that as his framework for the play of language. In doing so, he has abandoned the last remnants of traditional storytelling, still partially present in *The Hornets*. And yet the novel has all the trappings of its prototype—a style of formula writing full of stereotypical situations and language, including a murder, its detection, and attempted solution. Even the motto that precedes the story invokes Raymond Chandler, the old master of mystery. But here the similarities end. For each situation there is a sentence that functions as a Leibnitzian monad, a self-contained piece of information. There are no inherent connections between sentences or situations; no compelling nexus leads the reader through the mystery's stages. If there is to be a solution, the readers must supply the connective tissues of the plot. They must create the novel themselves, for its reality is one of process and not product.

The titles of the novel's twelve chapters sketch the developmental stages of the traditional mystery: "The order before the first disorder," "The first disorder," "Demasking the original order," "The order of the disorder," "The investigation," "The interrogation," "The apparent return to order and the lack of consequences before the second disorder," "The second disorder," "Mistaken detection," "Calm before the detection," "Detection," "The final return to order." Each chapter is divided into two sections. The first section, which is italicized, contains an analysis of the mystery as genre in essayistic form. The second section contains the actual mystery: a confusing disarray of fragmented perceptions, thoughts, quotations, and persons. An example illustrates Handke's style:

> On a day like this no one thinks of death. The handle of a shovel is sticking out of a pile of gravel. The street is not empty. The peddler sees a stone the size of a child's fist. His scalp contracts. No one wipes across his face quickly with a handkerchief. The sidewalk is fairly high above the street. The coat reaches all the way to the peddler's ankles. Soap suds force their way through a crack under a door. The bottle is floating almost upright in the water. Windows follow upon doors.
>
> He sees more clearly than otherwise. The fingernail scratches from cloth to buttons. The peddler moves his legs as if it were a natural act. The seat backs in the car form a perfect line. The street has recently been washed. He is surprised to see his own knees in front of him. The windows flicker. He shakes his head with a sense of disbelief. Only one shoe is shiny, the other is dusty. Thoughts overwhelm him. A nail was bent while pounding it in! (pp. 12–13)

Although randomly selected, this section can easily represent the way the novel generally proceeds. The apparent unconnectedness of these sentences stands in stark contrast to the clearly developed thoughts of the same chapter's first section:

> *The murder mystery conceals the true relationship of the described objects to each other. The story consists of playing with possible relationships of objects to each other. It consists of a hide-and-seek game of sentences. From the beginning, the murder mystery describes each object for itself. . . . The story begins with a person who is always just arriving, who never belongs there. The newly arrived person sees the things at the place of the action for the first time. He has to perceive them all.* (p. 8)

These analytical abstractions are contrasted to the unmediated and unrelated perceptions of the second sections, which are purely and totally concrete, displaying a world not yet exposed to the trials of comprehension. Thus, Handke's novel functions as a dialectical interplay between the concrete and the abstract, each supplementing and contradicting the other.

As in *The Hornets*, the characters of this novel remain as backdrops—even the peddler is unable to grasp the situations played out before him—while the chaotic world of things stands in the foreground. The novel is a collection of plot fragments that could conceivably be part of a mystery, but there is no order to them. The world of objects speaks, but its language is undecipherable. The novel's disorder is carefully arranged to reveal the disorder of things per se, of things unconnected by the act of conscious perception and selection. Handke's technique is again partly indebted to Robbe-Grillet's style of the *nouveau roman*, which portrays situations as if randomly filmed by a camera. Yet rather than rest as a museum of objects hygenically cleansed of all projectively human (and hence dynamic) characteristics—as does the language of Robbe-Grillet's own mystery novel, *The Erasers* (1953)—Handke's *Peddler* yearns to be unleashed in the reader's mind, where the dynamics of interpretation rightly take place. To this end, all the props necessary for a mystery are present, including numerous murder weapons —a knife, a revolver, a piece of telephone cable, a nylon stocking, a rope—each of which could be the key to a potential plot. But only the reader can create it. Like the peddler of the novel, the reader is a witness who is omnipresent and who is involved in a search for the "truth." Each situation, each disjointed fact is like a sign in an unknown language. Solving the murder is the process of creating a new syntax for the apparent chaos that the novel provides. The reader is asked to sift through the randomly ordered details, to question the sentences and situations, and to establish a logical connection between them.

Handke's novel exposes and destroys the clichéd reality of the mystery novel while leaving the genre itself intact. By constructing a fully artificial model of a typical mystery, he undermines only its stereotyped projection of reality as such, thus offering a new and more fully reliable sense of the real: a self-constructed realm in which the reader rebuilds the world firsthand, using as components the fragmentary perceptions that the novel contains. The reader cannot use the apperceptional framework already present in his consciousness, for the world encountered in *The Peddler* is too far removed from customary experience. Instead, each object, each sense perception must be related to another, as if the reader were starting from scratch. Instead of discovering the hidden causality of the typical mystery, the reader must work solely within probability, constructing the causal chain leading to an undetermined solution. *The Peddler's* world is a world *as it is,* still uninterpreted and unconnected by language and perception. Creating the mystery and solving it is thus the process of reexperiencing reality, projecting meaning and order in the world of things. Handke assists this process by supplying the emotional stimuli of fear, anxiety, horror, and pain—with no absolute connection, however, no concrete link to the world of objects and persons that the novel presents. Sentences such as "The line is busy!" or "It's the poker that is missing!" or "There! And there! And there!" or "The shoelaces are loose!" evoke an emotional content without supplying its context, thereby making realistic projections the business of the reader and not the writer.

Handke's *Peddler* is an experiment, and like most experiments it contains the inherent danger that it will fail to produce the desired results. What is intended as an intellectual exercise of the first order could be perceived as a task of deadening boredom. Like many experimental novels, *The Peddler* flaunts its intention, revels in its refusal to entertain, and assaults the reader's sensibilities in a spiteful kind of way. Whereas one reader might consider *The Peddler* nothing more than 120 pages of monotonous playing with language, another might praise Handke's ability to shape into fiction a steadfast refusal to engage the reader in a typical fashion.

The justification for Handke's antireaderly novel may be found in the book of shorter experiments he collected the same year, a volume that included several pieces written during his student days at Graz for Alfred Kolleritsch's magazine, *Manuskripte*. The texts within *Greeting the Board of Directors* combine straightforward narrative of personal experience with the strange and impersonal style that Handke continued to develop in his first two novels as well as in his plays. Alienation and estrangement are motifs common to the stories; fear, horror, violence, and destruction are, as in *The Peddler*, disembodied themes that are nevertheless constantly present.

In these early stories, Handke can already by found experimenting with literary models such as the mystery story ("The Peddler"), the wild-West story ("Sacramento" and "The Gallows Tree"), and the sanctified German *Bildungsroman* ("Between Sleeping and Waking"). By imitating these familiar genres and at the same time showing them to be models of reality, Handke indicates the artificiality or "constructedness" of narrative forms—and thus draws attention to the artificiality of all constructs. He sees this comprehension of constructs as the first stage in changing perception: by recognizing the world we live in as a mental construct, we take a first step toward changing that world. Here can be found the moral justification, if ever needed, for putting readers through the paces that a novel like *The Peddler* so brazenly demands.

The collection's title story takes for its foundation the metaphorical and ambiguous saying, "The beams are creaking" ("Es knistert im Gebälk"), a comment indicating deterioration, decay, and impending collapse. "Greeting the Board of Directors," reminiscent of Kafka's stories, portrays a dreamlike realm with its own logic, a strange and threatening world in which language is a vehicle of ambiguity. The story takes shape as the direct address of an unknown speaker to an undescribed board of directors. The speaker has called the members to an emergency meeting in a broken-down farmhouse in midwinter. He gives a threateningly ambiguous talk that exposes the manipulative character of language by constantly varying the phrase "the beams are creaking" and using it in different situations until it becomes evident that the beams are indeed creaking and doom is near: "The idea occurred to him [one of the members] that something might not be in order in the company, that the beams were creaking suspiciously. No, the beams are not creaking suspiciously (excuse me, what a storm!)" (p. 9). The last sentence, illustrating that the beams are indeed loudly creaking, nullifies the speaker's denial. Later he is forced to shout: "Come closer, otherwise you won't be able to hear anything. And on top of that, the beams are creaking" (pp. 9–10). It soon becomes evident that this sentence has two distinct meanings (concretely, that the beams of the old house are creaking; metaphorically, that decay in the corporation is evident) and that the speaker is intentionally using both meanings to his own advantage, manipulating the ambiguity of language in order to manipulate people.

In a number of the stories in *Greeting the Board of Directors,* Handke uses cinematic plot summaries in order to point out how films are often models of a clichéd reality. By recapitulating these movie plots in a brief space, Handke is able to show their lack of substance. Films often use preexisting, ritualized models of reality in both their stories and their characters, especially where they depict violence and death. Such forms, Handke argues, are scarcely creative, having become instead things in themselves, added to the world instead of representing it.

Several of the original stories later found their way into Handke's novels: "The Hornets," "The Flood," and "Outbreak of a War" were incorporated into *The Hornets,* while "The Peddler" is apparently a study leading to the novel of that name. The story "The Peddler" seems to be a sketch for a play or film script. Although story and novel share the title and both are framed as mysteries, there are few similarities between the two. In the story, a convicted murderer with a contract from an unknown source uses the identity of a peddler as a disguise to gain access to and kill a general. In "Between Sleeping and Waking (sketch for a *Bildungsroman*)," a parody of this hallowed German genre, a tough, ignorant, and generally unsavory character is constructed from the clichéd expressions of everyday speech—like the film stories and the murder mystery an example of narrative representing itself. Unlike the traditional *Bildungsroman,* in which the protagonist experiences the world as a learning and growing process leading to integration with society, the main character of "Between Sleeping and Waking" experiences negative *Bildung* (education, development); in turn, he rejects and is rejected by the society in which he lives. Instead of cultivating his innerworld, Handke's character "pays a lot of attention to his appearance" (p. 45). As if to stress this aspect of negative *Bildung* and so draw attention to the form as form, Handke begins the story with the sentence, "He closed his eyes," which thus negates the intention of cultivation and education implicit in the subtitle.

Handke's experiences as a law student find their expression in what is perhaps the anthology's strangest text, "Martial Law." Paragraph for paragraph, Handke reproduces, in only slightly altered form, a part of the penal code governing martial law. This is the kind of alienation effect preferred by Bertolt Brecht; by divorcing a thing (in this case a legal text) from its accustomed ambient and making just a few changes, the author allows the thing to be revealed for what it really is: strange, artificial, constructed, and questionable. In "I Am an Ivory Tower Dweller" Handke discusses the genesis of "Martial Law." "Some years ago," he recalls, "I found a statute concerning martial law in a book of criminal justice. In the form of paragraphs, the conditions governing the declaration of martial law in a given area are defined," with every action spelled out in painstaking detail: "how the court has to be constituted, how it is to act, what legal recourse is available to the accused, what sentence is to be handed down in a court under martial law (death)," and so on, right down to the most final matters, including "what is to happen after the passing of sentence (two hours after sentencing the sentence is to be carried out; upon request of the condemned, a third hour may be granted to prepare for death)" (p. 27). Such odd precision of language and such an "abstract form of describing a ritualized death" captivated Handke. "The logical consistency of the sentences, which were in essence always *conditional sentences* for a concrete, thinkable reality" revealed, in spite of the very abstractness of form, "a new possibility of viewing the phenomena of death and dying" (p. 28).

The coldly rational and emotionless language of legal documents is unmasked here and shown to be brutal, sadistic, and repressive. But as if the legal text itself were not threatening enough, Handke exaggerates certain clauses of the law to the extent that the story becomes a parody. His alterations allow rare glimpses of life to enter the text: "If the residents of the village are excluded from the proceedings because of their threatening behavior, then they are to be forbidden to look through their windows and through cracks in their sheds or barns. . . . If the proclamation [of the death penalty] cannot be heard due to the screaming of the residents, then it must be repeated. . . . Singly, the condemned step out of the doorway and raise their bound hands a little; the first of them then walks slowly across the yard to a wall. While turning around he spits" (p. 109). In this passage the author breaks open the perfected and closed form of a law that tolerates no exception. He reduces the abstract to the concrete by introducing specific examples of possible behavior. In doing so, he manages to expose this kind of law as a tautology that both excludes and precludes concrete examples of human activity. Life is reduced to clinically sterile formulas, squeezing out all humanity, if language is allowed to do its work transparently. But like Márquez, whose magic realism mixes probable and fantastic together, and like Barthelme, whose innovative fiction drops patently absurd items of content into the familiar forms of advertising and technological shoptalk, Handke wakes his readers to language's own reality by disrupting its smoothly familiar (and hence anesthetizing) flow.

"Martial Law," like many of the stories in *Greeting the Board of Directors,* is designed as a self-conscious model. The law in question is shown to be a highly artificial construct, a human artifact, and as such it is a thing to be questioned and perhaps changed. Both in intention and in style, these early texts presage Handke's later development as a novelist. The abstraction of representation evident in these stories and in his first two novels soon gives way to a more concrete and readable prose style that characterizes his mature work. Many of the themes typical of Handke's writing, including the philosophical and epistemological concerns that find their first expression in the texts of *Greeting the Board of Directors,* are carried over into his later fiction, in which they achieve fruition as complete and satisfying demonstrations of the semiotic process at work. For postmodern artists, man is the sign-making animal, and Handke's success in making his fiction self-apparent has helped put to rest those critical and exaggerated pronouncements concerning the alleged death of the novel.

III. The Death of the Death of the Novel

> The ticket tray next to the driver seemed open. Something like a glove lay in the center aisle of the bus. Cows were sleeping in the meadows next to the road. It was no use denying any of that.
>
> —*The Goalie's Anxiety at the Penalty Kick*

That Peter Handke's next novel would be his first to be translated into English and become an international best-seller is no accident, for it is the first evidence that his apprenticeship to the postmodern aesthetic was coming to an end and that his deconstructive death-of-the-novel phase was yielding to a more confident control of what positive elements had survived this purifying process. Moreover, audiences for this new style of literary work were growing. Thanks to the great popular successes of John Fowles's *French Lieutenant's Woman,* Kurt Vonnegut's *Slaughterhouse-Five* (both published in 1969), and Gabriel García Márquez's *One Hundred Years of Solitude* (the English-language translation of which appeared in 1970 and sold widely as a paperback beginning in 1971), British and American readers were being schooled in the lessons of innovative fiction—the same principles Peter Handke had been working out, in dogmatic fashion, within his earlier novels and stories. Rather than accepting fiction as a secondhand account of another reality, readers were beginning to demand that novels should be something validly real in themselves: not an illusionistic history of the world or a sociological model of it by which they could learn lessons to apply to life, but a life of fiction in itself—an addition to the world, not a representation of it.

The early 1970s, when Handke's fiction made its first appearance on the American scene, were years of great tumult for the traditions of novelistic art. Kurt Vonnegut,

Richard Brautigan, and Donald Barthelme had taken center stage, from bestseller lists through campus celebrity to regular appearances, in Barthelme's case, in the pages of *The New Yorker* magazine—all of which helped to create a mood of wider acceptance for the new styles of fiction. Novelist Ronald Sukenick's assessment of this change describes the broader field of action opened to readers and writers alike, once the limitations of a narrowly defined realism were eclipsed:

> The great advantage of fiction over history, journalism, or any other supposedly "factual" kind of writing is that it is an expressive medium. It transmits feeling, energy, excitement. Television can give us the news, fiction can best express our response to the news. No other medium— especially not film—can so well deal with our strongest and most often intimate responses to the large and small facts of our daily lives. But to do this successfully the novel must continually reinvent itself to remain in touch with the texture of our lives. It must make maximum expressive use of all elements of the printed page, including the relation of print to blank space. It must break through the literary formulas when necessary, while at the same time preserving what is essential to fiction: incident, feeling, power, scope, and the sense of consciousness struggling with circumstance.[1]

This broader field of activity is just what Handke's translated works of the early and mid-1970s address themselves to. Instead of arguing a thesis, as he had necessarily done in his earlier, formative works, he could now settle down to the more fluid practice of his beliefs, all of which made for easier going among readers and writer alike. From *The Goalie's Anxiety at the Penalty Kick* through *The Left-Handed Woman,* Handke would help to introduce American readers to that great renaissance in world writing that had been transforming their own national literature as well.[2]

Whereas *The Hornets, The Peddler,* and the stories from

1. Ronald Sukenick, "Innovative Fiction/Innovative Criteria: Reinventing the Novel," *Fiction International,* nos. 2–3 (1974): 133.

2. International coverage of this phenomenon is found in Raymond Federman, ed., *Surfiction* (Chicago: Swallow Press, 1975).

Greeting the Board of Directors were exercises in breaking down older assumptions about fiction, Handke's subsequent work could concentrate on building up a new reading experience within the axioms of postmodernism. There were indeed revolutions within language and reality to be considered, including the notion that when writing and reading we accept counterfeit representations as actual while we are in fact only dealing with degrees of difference among these representations, never with the things themselves. Such is the legacy of eighty years of linguistic debate, with which Handke's earlier work had reckoned in terms of fiction's most central conventions. But can there be human interest in all of this, particularly of the daily-life variety so natural to popular fiction? Can the novel tell us how people live and think and feel under such conditions? Can fiction incorporate its own sense of the provisional when it comes to the point of testing the relative merits of world-making systems, which are, after all, what linguistic structures really are? And, once the outmoded conventions of narrative have been tossed aside, is there material left to tell interesting and even compelling stories? It was to this second stage of the aesthetic revolution, when the death of the novel had become a dead issue, that Handke next addressed himself, with successes that would make him a renowned writer worldwide.

Handke's first achievement in facing this new, complex challenge was to devise a character whose daily life in the recognizable world embodies the linguistic crisis that has caused the rules for literary aesthetics to be rewritten. The protagonist of his third novel (and first to be translated into English), *The Goalie's Anxiety at the Penalty Kick* (1970, translated 1972), is Joseph Bloch, a former soccer goalie whose special perspective on language and reality matches the tactics of his play on the field. For Bloch, no action is simple. Noticing a circling hawk, he watches not "the hawk fluttering and diving, but the spot in the field for which the bird would presumably head" (p. 33). So too for the other things he comes across in life: Bloch tries to focus on the final object, not on the subjective action toward it. As the novel concludes, he explains this habit to a fellow spectator:

> "It's very difficult to take your eyes off the forwards and the ball and watch the goalie," Bloch said. "You have to tear yourself away from the ball; it's a completely unnatural thing to do." Instead of seeing the ball, you saw how the goalkeeper ran back and forth with his hands on his thighs, how he bent to the left and right and screamed at his defense. "Usually you don't notice him until the ball has been shot at the goal." (p. 132)

Hence the title's meaning: it is the goalie who feels anxiety, for his attention is riveted on the system behind each action, on *what may happen* rather than what is simply transpiring at hand. In the world of apparently substantial things, his life is one of the foggiest supposition; he has left his job, for example, assuming he has been fired, simply because no one but the foreman looks at him in the morning when he reports for work. In the linguistic terms that Handke favors for characterizing behavior, the goalie's world is one of ever-floating signifiers that may or may not attach themselves to objects that then become factors in the game. Reality must be actualized through language, and this is what makes Bloch rightfully uncertain. All is up in the air, and it is the goalie's fate to experience the anxiety that goal-keeping and language theory share.

Bloch therefore finds it hard to act at all, except in gratuitous ways. What would otherwise be a crisis—losing one's job—is here passed off without even a shrug of the shoulders, and may not have really happened at all. The most crucial act, in which Bloch murders a young woman, is seemingly unmotivated and has taken place in a world without consequence, so detached are his actions from any final signification. His consciousness having been separated from the world, he finds it hard even to worry about the police—"Again it seems to Bloch as if he were watching a music box: as though he had seen all this before" (p. 40). The only way he can endure the passing moments of life is to name objects, "thinking of the word for each thing" (p. 58) or, better yet, demanding to know its price. "With his eyes closed," we learn, "he was overcome by a strange inability to visualize anything," so tied to the system of language has he become. "He resorted to thinking up sentences about the things instead of words for them" (p.17), but even this narrative grammar leaves him in a world where the names seem more real than the things themselves. In Handke's fiction, phenomenological description (à la Robbe-Grillet) depletes itself in an exhaustion of naming:

> Next to him on the bench there was a dried-up snail spoor. The grass under the bench was wet with last night's dew; the cellophane wrapper of a cigarette box was fogged with mist. To his left he saw . . . To his right there was . . . Behind him he saw . . . He got hungry and walked away. (p. 77)

In such a world, details are like nameplates—"Neon signs," Bloch calls them. "So he saw the waitress's ear with one earring as a sign of the entire person." For every man or woman present, there is a detail to "stand for," "represent," or serve as "simile" (p. 88). This is not a happy state of affairs, and "the grating details seemed to stain and completely distort the figures and the surroundings they fitted into. The only defense was to name the things one by one and use those names as insults against the people themselves" for allowing such a system of signs to consume them (p. 89). The problem is Bloch's, for he can see the semiotic system (all too well!) but cannot naturally participate in it. Yet is there any other way to live, except on the surface of linguistic (and hence totally arbitrary) signification? Theorists from Saussure down through Derrida and Kristeva have shown how language never gives one custody of the thing in itself—only of a chimera bearing no real connection, a conventional fabrication of relationships. Still, that system is all we have to work with, as Bloch's maddeningly shallow life reveals. "He described events to himself like a radio announcer to the public, as if this was the only way he could see them for himself" (p.97). Language theorists would say he is absolutely right.

No necessary relationship between words and things, no licit grammar of action—this is what Bloch's behavior has proved, as he left a job he might not have been fired from and murdered a woman for no reason at all. *The Goalie's Anxiety,* however, is not a philosophical or linguistic treatise; it is a novel written out of the essentials of contemporary experience, and as Bloch flees the city for a southern border town he undertakes a life of hiding out, on the run, among the significations of a simpler social life. After all, it is the surface of reality he must manipulate in order to save himself. Reality as we experience it is created by language; hearing noise in the street, Bloch imagines a scene of garbagemen and rattling cans, which prevails as a vision of reality until his memory tells him it must be something else, since there is no garbage pickup in the country. In order to make sense of what he felt to be a strange encounter at work, Bloch had to assume he had been fired. Now, in order to survive, he must live totally on the surface, denying the deeper reality of himself as the murderer. He continues to energize existence on the simplest level, creating little of substance because nothing can be risked. In so doing, he expresses Peter Handke's stylized vision of the world, as uniquely characteristic as any passage from Dickens or Hawthorne and just as revealing of its author's view that for all practical purposes we live in a world of signs and not things:

> The waitress went behind the bar. Bloch put his hands on the table. The waitress bent down and opened the bottle. Bloch pushed the ashtray aside. The waitress took a cardboard coaster from another table as she passed it. Bloch pushed his chair back. The waitress took the glass, which had been slipped over the neck of the bottle, off the bottle, set the coaster on the table, put the glass on the coaster, tipped the beer into the glass, put the bottle on the table, and went away. It was starting up again. Bloch did not know what to do any more. (p. 34)

On this level, the safe level, all is predictable. All is boring, in fact, to the point of being maddening. The linguistic conventions Bloch practiced with the murdered woman were irritating—perhaps they were the reason he struck through the cardboard surface of "reality" to the unspeakable violence beneath. Bloch's hands take over the job of controlling reality when words fail, a common enough practice. When he doesn't act, or doesn't at least name things, he himself disappears.

Yet no man can ever win at this game. Naming things gives them life beyond themselves, to the extent they can no longer function in a grammar; every word gets boxed in quotes: " 'The chickens' 'peck at' 'grapes that had been dropped' " (p. 128). By the novel's end, Bloch is speaking in hieroglyphs, as representations of each object are blocked out across the page. Only by feinting no action, by standing completely still, can the goalie block the kick. In *The Goalie's Anxiety* Joseph Bloch has petrified himself in order to keep communication under his absolute control.

Although the fictional world of *The Goalie's Anxiety at the Penalty Kick* is bleak, it is only a provisional view—Handke's artistic response to a very real linguistic condition in the lives we all lead. Since its inception, fiction has been an alternative to life: a stylized if not idealized version, an *account* of reality that is more to be admired for how it changes things rather than keeps them the same. Certain masters have shown how this process can be therapeutic for author and audience alike—think of Tolstoy, or even more notably Hemingway. The latter's "Big Two-Hearted River" creates with painstaking realistic detail just such an alternative world, where all is ordered and measured in a way that soothes the shellshock of war's chaos. Fiction projects human design onto the things of this world, and its art is valued by how persuasive an account is rendered within the practice of artistic license. Postmodernism, of course, questions as means any attempt to anchor that persuasion on a fidelity to unexamined sign systems (in which the processes of signification are not taken into account); within his more constructive phase, however, Peter Handke has seen fit to consider whether the practice of fiction itself, and not just its content, can express this ideal.

For this reason, what happens in *The Goalie's Anxiety* is

less important than what the protagonist interprets as happening, as if he is the author of the world's text. In this way Handke shifts attention from the created to the creative world, from product to process. If all systems are fictions and if man is the sign-making animal as postmodern thought claims, the novel should not be judged by how accurately its world corresponds to ours but by how convincingly it presents Joseph Bloch's activity of putting his own world together. The only fair presumption of meaning is that there is no meaning at all until the protagonist initiates the process. Whether he has really been fired is immaterial, since 133 pages of narrative follow from the fact that he *thinks* he has been dismissed; if he had surmised the opposite, the novel's structure implies, the world that subsequently unfolds would be quite different. Only inanimate objects are "stark and unequivocal" (p. 15), as Bloch himself notes during an early scene, when a trumpet, neutral as a simple phenomenon, is transformed by the way a comic actor plays it. Without their human use, the things of this world are meaningless—introducing the element of the human into the world's affairs unleashes the play of signification that allows meanings to be attached however the user desires.

Awareness of this semiotic system makes every social act a self-consciously deliberate affair and provides Handke's novel with its rich substance. Merely to walk down the street is an adventure, and to have a conversation becomes an excruciatingly complex undertaking. Semiotic structures are everywhere, and Bloch is never safe from them no matter how hard he tries to distance himself. His anonymous relationship with the movie cashier becomes, despite his efforts to keep within himself, an interpersonal affair, since she talks about things he has mentioned "as if they were hers" (p. 19). Even after he has murdered her and fled to the anonymity of the south, Handke's protagonist finds it impossible to hide within his own speech; a conversation over lunch with a pair of shopgirls deteriorates into an unprovoked series of linguistic sallies: "Bloch noticed that each time he mentioned something and talked about it, the two of them countered with a story about their own experiences with the same or a similar thing or with a story they had heard about it" (p. 65), as if the young women feel they must identify themselves with the goalie's store of reality in order to exist themselves.

Signs for objects or for roles in the real world often seem more important than the objects or roles themselves. The woman who sells Bloch his paper at the newsstand every day, for example, pretends not to know him when they meet elsewhere on the street, and the bus driver on the trip south starts his engine "to signal that everybody else should get on board. . . . 'As if you couldn't understand him without that,' Bloch thought" (p. 29). Selecting his purchases at a general store, he learns that when he speaks casually in full grammatical sentences the clerk cannot understand him; to communicate effectively in his role as consumer he must name the objects he wants, one by one. Such naming is a contagious habit, for once his interest is sparked by the value attributed to an object he cannot rest until he knows the price of everything in sight. Before this passion ends, he is nearly driven to a frenzy by a storefront display in which there is no way to tell whether the price tag indicates a dress or the chair it rests on. Problems of meaning are ultimately problems of reading social signs, and as elements in a language signs have a life of their own; this makes simple existence all the more confusing, as when the landlady at the country inn switches on the radio. "When somebody in a movie turned on the radio, the program was instantly interrupted for a bulletin about a wanted man" (p. 114), and so Bloch cannot feel safe even though the act itself means nothing, so intimidating is its conventional structure.

Things by themselves may be innocent, but objects used in the world bespeak a summons to order that at times crushes Handke's protagonist, who by presuming he has lost his job has thereby lost step with the semiotic system of his world. Once cut off from this natural routine, every social act must be laboriously pieced together in a process like finding words in a foreign dictionary to complete a model sentence: "Back in town; back at the inn; back in his room. 'Eleven words altogether,' thought Bloch with relief" (p. 80). Yet it is such fresh attention to the signifying process, which is suddenly dramatic by virtue of Bloch's precarious position in it, that helps to unify the novel and make it a coherent human narrative. That Bloch's wanderings are inconclusive is not the point, for it matters not *where* he goes but *how,* attending to the semiotic processes of life all the way.

As we shall see in Chapter V, Handke has found this sense of linguistic adventure to be possible in drama, but as isolated acts of signification; only a novel provides the range of activity needed for their full display as the determining elements of social life. For Bloch to settle into reality he must become like Handke's beleaguered figure in *Kaspar,* who responds to commands from the play's prompters: "Everything fell into place: everywhere he saw a summons: to do one thing, not to do another" (p. 117), even to the point that spice boxes on the shelves and jelly in the jar spell out commands to him. Nor is this an unwelcome process; as with the price tags of objects, man has a compelling need to read for meaning. As does the play *Quodlibet,* Handke's novel provides nonsensical utterings taken as mispronunciations; so great is our quest for readability and meaning that we create order from verbal chaos. Bloch's fear of discovery, for example, teases him into hearing "got to remember" and "why watch?" from two policemen who really say "goats you remember" and "whitewash." In our quest for signs, even sounds cannot be left for themselves. To be happy, we must make them mean something, however artificial or paranoid that process might turn out to be. But in Handke's world, such needs are not always answered, just as signification is not an automatic process—like any thing of artifice, it can run afoul (producing misunderstanding) or pull up incomplete (when communication is blocked). In the novel's southern village, a mute schoolboy has disappeared, and the search for him is hampered by his inability to call for help, a reminder of Handke's similarly defined dramatic piece *Calling for Help,* in which the actors are able to cry for everything except the word *help.* Indeed, the janitor of the village school claims that all the children, "more or less, have a speech defect," since "they couldn't manage even to finish a single sentence of their own, they talked to each other almost entirely in single words, and they wouldn't talk at all unless you asked them to, and what they learned was only memorized stuff that they rattled off by rote" (p. 104). With no workable grammar, the village provides the goalie with an apt example of language in its most problematic state.

Yet the great human drama of interpretation remains, not only providing Handke with a theme but giving him a natural structure for his novel. As a goalie, Bloch's job during the penalty kick was to avoid telegraphing any sign whatsoever to the other team's forward and so prevent him from anticipating the goalie's move to block. When the border guard who accompanies the goalie back to town spots a hedgehog in the dark, he satisfies Bloch's amazement by advising, "That's part of my profession. Even if all you see is one movement or hear just one noise, you must be able to identify the thing that made that movement or sound" (p. 119). Facing off against a suspect who might try to escape, the guard reveals, demands the same ability to feint one's own moves and read the other's: "It's important to look the other guy in the eyes. Before he starts to run, his eyes show which direction he'll take. But you've also got to watch his legs at the same time. Which leg is he putting his weight on?" (p. 121). Throughout the novel Bloch has been thinking in just such terms, from his strategy for the penalty kick to the ways he studies the ground below a circling hawk or the coaster beneath a trickling drop of condensation on a beer mug. If something falls, Bloch is there to catch it; if something is lost, he feels compelled to find it. His success in all these endeavors is due to his ability to freeze the semiotic process and examine it as a thing in itself, rather than blandly let it run its routine course and thereby, for all practical matters, disappear.

The careful reader will note that subliminally the novel has been held together by the same technique of free-floating signs that by nature are directed toward some type of meaning: the sound of "a stone on a dirt road slamming against the bottom of a car" occurs, free of any objective signification, during the strangling scene (p. 20) and then again on a ride to the border (p. 107); a black purse sits on a village windowsill (p. 53) and later on a cafe table (p. 67); various items are caught just before they fall—and so forth, through a series of unattached references that through their very liberty from meaning prompt the reader's desire to make them connect. Throughout, the signifying process is kept open and therefore alive, avoiding the closure of meaning appropriate to a strictly realistic novel. In this way, Bloch sustains his own freedom and Handke revitalizes a key convention of narrative art.

Handke's fourth novel (and second translated into English) turns to other conventions—not simply linguistic, but now geographical and historical—to remake postmodern fiction along these lines. *Short Letter, Long Farewell* (1972, translated 1974) gives us a narrator closely similar to Handke himself, right down to nationality, age, and family background, who is traveling across the United States pursued by the complications of an unhappy marriage. Like a Hemingway character in search of fictional solace, he is deeply troubled and wanders through this stage of life looking for meaningful order. "As far back as I can remember," he begins, "I seem to have been born for horror and fear" (p. 3). As with the Hemingway hero, these feelings are debilitating and complicate enjoyment of life. He can neither relate to other people nor rest within himself; the stormy relationship with his estranged wife, Judith, is recalled on nearly every page, and she haunts his restless progress from town to town and from image to image. But here is where Handke's life of fiction finds help rather than hindrance in how the world is organized. In *The Goalie's Anxiety*, linguistics proved an obstacle—or seemed so at the root of Joseph Bloch's problem. In *Short Letter*, however, Handke's narrator finds that another system—world geography and the peculiar relationship of America to Europe—provides an image of resolution as effective as any of Hemingway's alternatives (sports and heroics), yet without demanding any suspension of disbelief or secondhand representations of reality.

For Handke's Austrian narrator, America is real and unreal all at the same time. As the "new" world, it is a provisional reenactment of the old. For a man of troubled intellect, it is invitingly Platonic, having sprung fully formed from the minds of its makers. Moreover, in a world foundering in linguistic confusion between sign and reality, America possesses a special *significant* nature. As his American friend tells him, "We, all of us here, learned to see in terms of historical pictures. A landscape had meaning only if something historical happened in it. A giant oak tree in itself wasn't a picture; it became a picture only in association with something else"—which recalls Handke's point that we know things only in terms of comparison—"for instance, if the Mormons had camped under it on their way to the Great Salt Lake." Only in America is the habit of linguistic naming, of the sign-making so debilitating to Bloch in *The Goalie's Anxiety*, a fully natural part of the order, readily acknowledged as such: "Every view of a canyon might just as well have a sentence from the Constitution under it" (p. 101). The same is true for historical figures referred to in these signs: "For us they haven't any biography, they're trademarks for what they did or what was done in their day, we're not interested in their lives. We remember them as they appear in monuments and postage stamps" (p. 125). And so the signs are most emphatically not references to something else; they are themselves, and dominate the cultural landscape from decorative design schemes and restaurant motifs to paintings and films, forever reminding the viewer who and where he is. "Nothing is made up," director John Ford tells the narrator at the end. "It all really happened" (p. 165).

If Joseph Bloch had come to America instead of to the Austrian border town, he might have had an easier time. Indeed, as a world-class soccer player, Bloch had traveled to the United States often and still carries American money with him. For Handke's narrator in *Short Letter*, the States are a happy place; his own pathological examination of the relationship between ideas and things is accommodated in the country's daily ritual. By means of his transient life among hotels, motels, roadside restaurants, and a traveler's geography that changes every day, he is able to be acutely sensitive to the American topology of endless highways and tourist attractions. In this sense, *Short Letter's* closest rival is that other foreign traveler's celebration of America's tantalizing surfaces, Vladimir Nabokov's *Lolita*. Handke's narrator is special, however, because he has, in a sense, become free of language and is envied for it. "I haven't got an America I can go away to like you," his American friend complains (p. 66).

Yet Americans do travel imaginatively from the day-to-day reality of their land, which Handke judges as a place of self-apparent surfaces. What you see is what there is. Seeing everything as a sign for itself, idealizing the country's history in each cross-country drive, celebrating the land's self-conscious identity at every mundane occasion: this is the imaginative re-invention of reality that Handke's narrator encounters at every turn and that he sees expressed so well in American literature. In fact, the narrator finds it hard to exist outside these images, as if the real America is within and not behind them. Booking a hotel room in New York, he is drawn to the Algonquin because F. Scott Fitzgerald immortalized it through his residencies there. Then comes a reading of *The Great Gatsby* itself as the narrator tries to immortalize his every act: "The great Gatsby now commanded me to transform myself instantly" (p. 11). A Tarzan film makes him relive his youth; the four-panel structure of a Peanuts comic strip begins to shape his life, as "I had the feeling that in every fourth frame my feet were pulled out from under me and I fell flat on my face. And then another adventure story started up!" (p. 28). Movie stars—Buster Keaton, Marilyn Monroe, Stan Laurel—become, as they are for many Americans, exemplars of life. And so the narrator's own cross-country journey, mimicking a pioneer's trek, leads inevitably to the American celluloid mythmaker, the legendary director of historical epics, John Ford.

As his American travels continue, the narrator "noticed that little by little I was beginning to take in the surroundings without any sense of strain" (p. 16). In this manner, *Short Letter* begins with a resolution of the problems with which *The Goalie's Anxiety* had concluded. There is still a bit of labored description to get things underway, such as a walk down New York's Park Avenue in which "I compulsively described all the partial actions of which the total action was composed" (p. 25), but this is simply to establish the rhythm so natural to Americans—a rhythm the narrator captures "by dissecting the few activities within my reach as though speaking of momentous undertakings" (p. 26). He soon internalizes the urban landscape ("It was pleasant: the pattern of New York spread out peacefully inside me"), and the act of naming becomes natural and easy, like reading a menu. "I wanted to lie down in it," the narrator confesses, "and read a book" (p. 37).

He has been reading a novel, Gottfried Keller's *Der grüne Heinrich,*[3] in which the protagonist's vision is as twisted as that of Handke's narrator had been:

> When I tried to describe something, I never knew what it looked like; I remembered only its anomalies, and if there weren't any, I made them up. All the people I described were giants with birthmarks and falsetto voices. Most often they were escaped convicts, who sat for hours on tree trunks in the woods, telling their stories to the wind. I was quick to see cripples, blind men, and idiots, but even these I could not have described in detail. I was more interested in ruins than in houses. I liked to spend my time in graveyards and always counted the suicides' graves along the wall. (pp. 52–53)

Now, however, he is in a land that has solved the linguistic problem, a land that lives easily with the unbridgeable gap between signifier and signified. America, where signs are nothing but themselves, is the land of experimental realism, and Handke's narrator delights in it. He reads an American newspaper, and "whatever I saw in print aroused a compulsive sympathy in me; I felt drawn to every place or person

3. Ralph Manheim half-translates this title as *Green Heinrich.*

mentioned" (p. 31). What has been his problem in the past? Simply an inability to live in harmony with the linguistic structures of existence, which consist of endless comparisons rather than of things in themselves. "I've come to understand since I've been here, why the only memory I ever developed was for frightening things," he says. "I never had anything with which to compare the things I saw every day. All my impressions were repetitions of impressions that were already known to me," making his participation in the play of signs a very limited affair. "It wasn't just that I didn't get around much, but also that I didn't see many people whose circumstances were different from mine. Since we were poor, nearly all the people I knew were poor." With few comparisons, there is little language. "We saw so few things that there was very little to talk about and we had the same conversation almost every day" (p. 61). Following this rural childhood came his boarding school years, "almost completely cut off from the outside world," in a place where so many things were forbidden that "the prohibitions formed a *system*" that enabled him later, "when experience was open to me, to experience them *systematically*, to classify my experiences, to know which experiences were still lacking, not to mistake one for another, in short, to avoid going mad" (pp. 104–5). These are the circumstances, and the traumas, of Joseph Bloch. America is, however, the land of opportunity, and the land in which endlessly new details are enchanting rather than threatening because they are all clearly labeled—and indeed are themselves the labels by which they are identified. America is a fully provisional land, with every signification self-apparent.

As the American dream provided Jay Gatsby with a grammar by which he could relate his ideals to objectively existing things and thereby create himself, so does the contemporary American reality—based as it is on self-apparent signs—allow Handke's narrator to construct a system of relationships by which he can realize his own identity, which has heretofore been lost amid anxious uncertainties. His American girlfriend, Claire, with whom he discusses his reading of *Der grüne Heinrich* as they travel, points out that Keller's protagonist has much in common with Handke's: "All he wanted was to be as detached as possible. . . . He let experience pass before his eyes and never got involved; the people he knew just danced by him," just as the narrator's life has prior to the revelation of his American travels. This is not really living, since "he made no attempt to decipher anything; one event would simply follow from another. . . . As if life were taking place on a stage and there was no need for you to get mixed up in it" (p. 80).

But life without such decoding is by definition a life without meaning, as the narrator learns from watching Claire's child and her attachment to personal objects. "What made her cling to things was fear," Claire explains; a panic overtakes children "when suddenly something that belonged to them a moment ago is somewhere else and the place it occupied is empty, and the reason is that when that happens they don't know where they themselves belong" (p. 71). On the other hand, the creative appropriation of the world's objects helps to form an identity, such as the insular relationship shared by Claire's friends in St. Louis, who are "so engrossed in each other that the most trifling objects that had accumulated in the course of their life together became as precious to them as the parts of their own body," because "only in the midst of these objects . . . could they be sure of remaining themselves" (p. 95). To keep the grammar of their relationship fresh, every act is performed as if for the first time, even though the world they have constructed is a perfectly self-sufficient state.

The narrator's marital relationship has been just the opposite, as objects and routines became excuses for hostility. Judith had been his first real experience outside himself, and, hence, when that relationship went bad the two of them "wanted to obliterate and destroy each other" (p. 113)—and so she stalks him now, from city to city, with threatening notes and devices. Her method is to activate malignantly the world her husband passes through, from a birthday card that states this one will be his last, through the local toughs she hires to rob and rough him up, to the picture postcard of their penultimate destination on the Oregon coast where she has determined that she will shoot him, dead.

To save himself he must write the final chapter of their relationship as a constructive rather than destructive narrative, and to do that he must put himself in better touch with life. "It must be possible for two human beings to belong to each other, to establish a relationship that is not personal, fortuitous, and ephemeral," he reflects, "not based on a fraudulent and continually exhorted love, but on a necessary, impersonal bond" (pp. 140–41). His American travels, from the Northeast across the continent to St. Louis and then from Arizona to the Pacific Northwest, have put him in touch with a wide, complex world for the first time—but at this point he must ask himself why "was it possible for me to lose myself in objects, but not in people!" (p. 140). As the novel nears its end, he can for the first time seriously question this aspect of himself that has kept him estranged: "Why had I never managed to be as unreflectingly loving to Judith as I was now while looking at this church dome or at the drops of wax on the stone floor?" (p. 141). But to relate this way demands the formulation of a language he has never before learned. "I realized how concerned I had always been with myself, to the exclusion of almost everything else, because I often didn't know what the things we saw were. For the first time it occurred to me that I had no words for some of the most common movements about me" (p. 98). And so his travels in America, where what you see is what there is, become a helpful first step toward establishing a grammar of relationship with the world.

And this lesson from his travels becomes the message that Handke's narrator, now joined by the transformed Judith whom he has faced and disarmed, decides to carry to John Ford in California: that his films have "taught me to understand history by seeing people in nature" (p. 116), history being the sum total of life's events to which the narrator had been previously unable to relate. To emphasize how America and its most typical art form, Hollywood movies, have made this breakthrough possible, Handke has his narrator stop for a performance by a German touring company of Schiller's *Don Carlos,* in St. Louis—a production that fails, because unlike John Ford's work, "Schiller isn't portraying historical figures but himself; under their names, he acts out the adventures into which they themselves put so little charm and dignity" (p. 125). Unlike John Ford's egalitarian America where men are equal as men and signs are simply themselves, "In Schiller's Europe only princes could be historical figures, and only historical figures could play roles and have adventures" (p. 126). Handke's narrator confesses to the same problem with a play he has been writing: "As soon as somebody says something, if only with a gesture, the character is reduced to a concept and I can't do anything more with him" (p. 128).

And so the broad sweep of an American novel suggests a doubly successful solution to the narrator's problems. He can feel sympathy for the American landscape as he watches from his motel window to become one with a cyprus tree swaying in the breeze. He can in similar manner be caught up within a John Ford epic, *The Iron Horse,* waiting for the transcontinental railroad and the two lovers, finally, to meet: "My whole body hungered for the two of them to come together" (p. 83). In such identifications, "I lost forever my longing to be rid of myself," he notes. "I knew that I would never again want to be rid of all those limitations, and that from then on only one thing would be important: to fit them all into an order and mode of life that would do me justice and enable others to do me justice" (p. 84).

This link between personal experience and the outside world, so elusive for Handke's characters, has been achieved by finding in America a still valid system of myth that incorporates particular objects and actions within a functional system of signification, thus providing a meaningful whole. Such a working myth, which here must be sought out half a world away from his Austrian homeland, will continue to be a compelling force in Handke's work, from his radical attacks on the outmoded forms of conventional literature to his own imaginative (and eventually physical) journey home. It is one thing to notice that a tree "swayed back and forth in a movement that resembled my own breathing" but quite another to experience the feeling that "the cypress, still gently swaying, moved closer with every breath and finally penetrated my chest. . . . I felt that the movement of the cypress was taking over the function of my respiratory center, making me sway with it, and freeing itself from me" (pp. 78–79.) Such an experience, which anticipates the climax of Handke's almost mystical novel *The Lesson of Sainte Victoire* (1980), speaks for the difference between metaphorical representation and genuine identification—a process Handke's narrator has in *Short Letter* found possible within America's self-apparency of signs.

Talking of his achievements to the narrator and his wife—who have agreed to seek their independent destinies, freed from the hostile relationship that nearly consumed them—John Ford explains the pluralism of American culture that extends even to its habits of grammatical usage: " 'We Americans always say "we" even when we're talking about our private affairs,' said John Ford. 'Maybe it's because we see everything we do as part of a common effort. "I" stories are possible only when one stands for all. We don't take our egos as seriously as you Europeans' " (p. 161). Hence, it is not surprising that Ford has achieved a sense of personal peace, to which he confesses as he watches the sun set across his California valley: "It gives me a feeling of eternity, and I forget that there's such a thing as history. You people call it a medieval feeling. It's as if the whole world were still in a state of nature" (p. 162).

For John Ford there are no confusions in his world, because there are no contradictions between story and event; in his mythic America, the story is an event in its own right. The scenic painter whom Handke's narrator met in St. Louis had achieved the same perfection in his art, simply by painting events whose significance in American culture provided them with their own legitimacy: in these terms a work like *Washington Crossing the Delaware* is less a representation of General Washington being rowed across the Delaware River than it is something in itself, a sign of what

America *is.* "The copy had replaced the original forever" (p. 99), just as Judith and the narrator can assure John Ford that their story is now their own reality; in telling it, the narrator has produced the book we now read and from which he himself has been freed.

Finally in touch with the network of things, the narrator can escape himself and feel sympathy for others—notably for his friend's child, for whom "the artificial signs and objects of civilization had become nature." She is the American who will inherit the future, and be happy with it, because the signs she encounters "stood for themselves" (p. 99). What the soccer goalie was unable to accomplish, she does naturally, thus becoming the vehicle for the narrator's successful accommodation to the world.

* * *

A Sorrow Beyond Dreams (1972, translated 1974) is Handke's demonstration that his complex fictional structures as perfected in *The Goalie's Anxiety* and *Short Letter* can bear the test of real life and that they have the same integrity when applied to the most personal of experiences. Subtitled *A Life Story,* this brief prose work (of about 19,000 words) occasioned by his mother's suicide in 1971 demands a reversal of Handke's customary posture as a writer, although his attention to structure assures that the effects are much the same. Here, he himself must compose the world, as before his protagonists have had to:

> Ordinarily, I start with myself and my own headaches; in the course of my writing, I detach myself from them more and more, and then, in the end, I ship myself and my headaches off to market as a commodity—but in this case, since I am only a writer and can't take the role of the *person written about,* such detachment is impossible. I can only move myself into the distance; my mother can never become for me, as I can for myself, a wingèd art object flying serenely through the air. She refuses to be isolated and remains unfathomable; my sentences crash in the darkness and lie scattered on the paper. (p. 30)

The subject is familiar, "about the nameless, about the speechless moments of terror." Most of all, "It is a record of states, not a well-rounded story with an anticipated, hence comforting, end" (pp. 30–31). Therefore, Handke's familiar activity of destroying the conventions of fiction restores literary prose to life by establishing writing's validity per se. "Having something to do brings me back to life" (p. 5), Handke admits at the beginning, and as his epigraph from Bob Dylan reminds us, "He not busy being born is busy dying."

Handke's prose meditation works to recreate his mother's feelings—to share them by submitting himself to a recollection of the determining objects in her life, which he arranges in a chronological narrative from birth to death. Shifting in and out of focus are key vignettes—of village life, time in the city, motherhood, abortions, and the like—that summarize her life. Along the way Handke uses techniques conventional to fiction—imagery, symbolism, point of view—and applies them most dramatically to real material.

The world of Peter Handke's mother proves to be, upon inspection, much like the world his characters have inhabited since his first novel. So many similar lives have been led that actions have become predictable; and so many of these lives have been circumscribed within close limits that the range of possible reactions is virtually determinate—so much so that signifying labels have been attached to them, in turn, making them no longer actions in themselves but rather signs for the general process of life. Even her pedigree is contaminated by sign-making, as her father's habits belie: "He continued to save toward the day when his children would need SETTLEMENTS, for marriage or to set themselves up in a trade. The idea that any of his savings might be spent before then on their EDUCATION couldn't possibly have entered his mind, especially where his daughters were concerned" (p. 8). And so Handke's mother is destined for a world of mechanical significations, in which she is merely one sign among others, the GOOD MOTHER, keeper of the hearth, existing as one among a world of objects, named by their characteristics:

> the GOOD OLD ironing board, the COZY hearth, the often-mended cooking pots, the DANGEROUS poker, the STURDY wheelbarrow, the ENTERPRISING weedcutter, the SHINING BRIGHT knives, which over the years had been ground to a vanishing point by the BURLY scissors grinders, the FIENDISH thimble, the STUPID darning egg, the CLUMSY OLD flatiron, which provided variety by having to be put back on the stove every so often, and finally the PRIZE PIECE, the foot-and-hand-operated Singer sewing machine. But the golden haze is all in the manner of listing. (pp. 41–42)

His mother's life is described by these objects. "You couldn't help becoming dependent on those things," Handke writes. Indeed, "There was nothing else." Because experiences and possibilities are limited, so is language; and, therefore, so is the range of human existence. "No possibilities of comparison with a different way of life: richer? less hemmed in?" (p. 11). There are no possibilities, just "the always identical objects around her, in always the same places!" (p. 49).

Information theory as propounded by Abraham Moles teaches that a maximum of intelligibility yields a minimum of information, precisely because of the dearth of intelligibly contrastive material. So too do the lives of rural Austrian women (such as Handke's mother) fade into nonbeing: "Tired/Exhausted/Sick/Dying/Dead," as the girls of their village play games with the stations of a woman's life. In "the bourgeois system of emotional relations," clichés become binding rules, simply because nothing else has been thought of; there is no answer to the question, Is there any other way to live? Life consists of types. "In the midst of these consoling fetishes, you ceased to exist. And because your days were spent in unchanging associations with the same things, they became sacred to you; not leisure, but work was sweet. Besides, there was nothing else" (p. 34). Their class as a whole disappears, effaced by an official language that replaces the repulsive sounding *paupers* with the more reclaimed and cleansed term *poor*: "Their life became so unimaginably abstract that they could be forgotten" (p. 39).

The process of signification is so strong that words create their own reality, alternately disguising or overemphasizing the true state of affairs. Recalling the primitive conditions in his village, Handke remarks that certain households owned but a single bowl, which would serve as a chamberpot by night and then be used for mixing bread dough the following day. Since the bowl was washed in boiling water, little harm could in fact be done. "The dual use of the bowl became disgusting," Handke emphasizes, "only when it was *described*: 'They relieve themselves in the same bowl they eat out of.'—'Ugh!' " In this instance, the signifier takes on a life apart from the signified in terms of effective meaning, as "words convey this sort of passive, complacent disgust much better than the sight of the phenomena they refer to" (p. 39). Handke thus avoids the rehearsals of abject misery that typify conventionally realistic narratives, because plain meaning often contradicts the sense of a "realist's" language. "Hence my distaste for descriptions of misery," he confesses, "for in hygienic, but equally miserable poverty, there is nothing to describe" (p. 40).

Language can just as easily abstract meaning so thoroughly that no real substance remains. The best examples are the catchwords of the author's childhood schoolbooks, in which terms were severed from any sense of tangible reality and related instead to images "devoid of human content: oppression as chains or boot heel, freedom as mountaintop, the economic system as a reassuringly smoking factory chimney or as a pipe enjoyed after the day's work" (p. 15). The process continued through the whole civic and social structure of Austrian life as perceived from his rural province. These formulations are part of the conditioning process by which societies manage to run smoothly, but the result is that the forms assume a greater functional reality than the recorded facts—and in just this way has his mother's life been destroyed. "Clichés are taken as binding rules," Handke notes, "and any *individual* reaction, which takes some account of an actual person, becomes a deviation." Even more insidiously, as people are forced to live within stereotypical forms, they begin to accept them as secure identities:

> And so this typology became a guide to life; it gave you a pleasantly objective feeling about yourself; you stopped worrying about your origins, your possibly dandruff-ridden, sweaty-footed individuality, or the daily renewed problems of how to go on living; being a type relieved the human molecule of his humiliating loneliness and isolation; he lost himself, yet now and then he was somebody, if only briefly. (p. 26)

But living within such forms rather than acknowledging the ever-changing flow of life creates an existence-in-stasis: "there was no need to involve *people*" in one's formulations because "*objects* suffice" (p. 34).

Reviewing the events of his mother's life, Handke finds few that speak for human originality: nearly everything, from her pleadings for her drunkard husband to her marital standoffs when he egregiously misbehaved, became "the old story" (p. 21), "an old story interchangeable with other old stories; unrelated to the time when it took place; in short, it smacks of the nineteenth century" (p. 38). Her only chance for transformation had been when the country itself was transformed on 10 April 1938, with "the Yes to Germany!" Handke reports his mother's excitement at the promise of a new life in which "everything that was strange and incomprehensible in the world took on new meaning and became part of a larger context" (p. 14). In fact, however, only the typology has been enlarged, from the Austrian Republic to the Third Reich, and even though it momentarily "enhanced people's sense of self" (p. 16), such political and military typologies were subject to sweeping defeat by the higher abstractions of history. The one love of her life was sealed within this passing romantic period, and soon the realities of defeat returned her to a lifetime sentence within the prewar village clichés. The grand hopes of 1938, based as they were on an external formulation, had only been a passing fashion.

As a life story, *A Sorrow Beyond Dreams* presents Handke with an even more serious challenge than the claims of novelistic exhaustion he faced in *The Hornets* and *The Peddler*, for in it he must create a personally meaningful narrative out of material whose very typicality threatens to efface itself into nothingness: his mother's story is so predictably determined that its routine telling would constitute no real story at all. Yet the mother-child relationship is nature's most intimate, and the act of suicide human nature's most personal, so the author must find some way to express his feelings—implied by the typologies of life to be fully unexceptional and therefore unworthy of narrative attention. Yet here is where Handke's self-conscious attention to the life of signs makes writing possible. After running through the basic facts of her life, which takes just less than half of his book's pages, Handke stops to consider what will be necessary for him to find the essentials of his mother's life and therefore justify his writing. He simply cannot dispassionately record what has happened, for that by itself would be history; nor can he allow his mother's individuality to become "painlessly submerged in poetic sentences" (p. 28), for that would be a lyricism more reflective of the author's feelings than of the narrative he wishes to engage. To keep his balance he must constantly renegotiate the terms by which individuals express their relation to existence, which means self-consciously attending to the signification process by which his mother identified herself in the world and by which Handke writes his story.

Therefore, he will start "not with the facts but with the already available formulations, the linguistic deposit of man's social experience," using the "ready-made public language" to sort out the individually relevant aspects of his mother's life. Sentence by sentence, then, Handke compares "the stock of formulas applicable to the biography of a woman with my mother's particular life; the actual work of writing follows from the agreements and contradictions between them." Anything that looks like a quotation is dropped, to avoid sending the narrative into predictable forms and implying aesthetic exhaustion. "Only if a sentence is firmly and circumspectly centered on my personal, or if you will, private subject," Handke promises himself, "do I feel that I can use it" (p. 29).

Although Peter Handke's mother may have been the victim of determining cultural illusions, the author insists that his own writing will not be so influenced. Therefore, he must maintain an absolute consciousness of typological forms so that his own text will not be swallowed up by them, which is what might happen if he surrendered to his materials and let the story tell itself. *A Sorrow Beyond Dreams* begins with Handke's frank confession of an overwhelming need to write the book at hand, an act that focuses the reader's attention on the volume itself rather than on the events about to unfold. Postmodern theory has emphasized that *to write* is an intransitive verb. "Language cannot be considered as a simple instrument, whether utilitarian or decorative, of thought," Roland Barthes explains, justifying his belief that "man does not exist prior to language, either as a species or an individual."[4] Writing is more than self-expression—it is self-definition, but this strengthening of the writer as subject also enhances the power of what is written. As Barthes concludes, "It was particularly at the moment when the verb *to write* appeared to become intransitive that its object, the book or the text, took on a particular importance."[5] In making a literary response to his mother's death, Handke reaffirms that the important point is not what is written *about* but what is produced by the *act* of writing—a decision especially significant to this situation in which both occasion and execution are threatened by the absence of any subject to explain.

"What I feel is not so much horror as unreality" (p. 4), Handke explains, and it is the need to formulate these "moments of extreme speechlessness" that "has led men to write from time immemorial" (p. 6). Writing is justified, in

4. Roland Barthes, "To Write: An Intransitive Verb?" *The Languages of Criticism and the Sciences of Man*, ed. Richard Macksey and Eugenio Donato (Baltimore: Johns Hopkins University Press, 1970), p. 135

5. Ibid., p. 142.

other words, when its reality can take no other form. At his mother's graveside in the book's closing scene, Handke looks around and is reminded, "Nature was really merciless. So these were the facts! The forest spoke for itself. Apart from these countless treetops, nothing counted." Without language there can be no naming, no enumeration, no structuring of sense; indeed, without language his mother would not exist. It is precisely because the tyranny of the world makes him feel so "mocked and helpless" that "in my impotent rage, I felt the need of writing something about my mother" (p. 66). Only in this way, when the process of writing becomes an act in itself, is the mute power of nature answered. "Obviously narration is an act of memory," but it "derives a little pleasure from the states of dread by trying to formulate them as aptly as possible; from enjoyment of horror it produces enjoyment of memory" (p. 67), which *A Sorrow Beyond Dreams* addresses as a self-apparent form. As an attempt to represent reality, the work accomplishes nothing; as an exercise in achieving something real in itself, the book succeeds. Handke says near the beginning of the book that because what he is "going through is incomprehensible and incommunicable," he is able to make "the horror seem meaningful and real" (p. 4) as an act of writing and not reporting.

Handke's insight is less simply into his mother than into the system that produced her, destroyed her, and has now provided the framework for his own literary self-examination. What has she died of? A "BROKEN HEART" (p. 52), the systemization that not only explains her failure but comforts her son and lets him end his narrative: "THAT DOES IT, THAT DOES IT, THAT DOES IT. GOOD, GOOD, GOOD" (p. 63). All follows naturally, right through to the funeral: "Only her name had to be inserted in the religious formulas" (p. 65). These are the facts, which Handke's fictional style suitably rescues for personal prose. In an age that has proclaimed the death of the novel, his writing has once more proved adequate for life.

For Peter Handke to tell his mother's story self-reflexively as an act of his own writing shows that *A Sorrow Beyond Dreams* draws its credibility not from the product but from the process displayed. Previously his fictional characters had been in flight from one self-definition or in search of another: in each case a self-conscious undertaking, but neither complete in itself as a narrative action. To see the world engaged at every step, one must turn to Handke's next two novels, for which the semiotic processes described so well in *The Goalie's Anxiety at the Penalty Kick* and *Short Letter, Long Farewell* become the premise for a more complexly developed narrative action, covering fully characterized individuals in virtually every aspect of their daily life.

Handke's fully mature voice as a novelist finds expression in *A Moment of True Feeling* (1975, translated 1977) and *The Left-Handed Woman* (1976, translated 1978). These are complete novels, in the sense of being complex human actions worked out within a social context to full resolution. *The Goalie's Anxiety* provides a linguistic basis for their actions, which can now be confidently assumed rather than laboriously tested out. The mechanically narrative structure of *Short Letter* is in these two books handled more naturally, as their protagonists' lives develop in a day-to-day manner, without benefit or need of an elaborate travelogue to move time along. Most of all, the deeply personal emotion of *A Sorrow Beyond Dreams*—which was, after all, a narrative memoir and not a work of fiction—is here successfully applied to imaginatively created situations. The respective characters, Gregor and Marianne, are among Handke's most deeply realized, and his triumph has been to make them convincing without sacrificing any of his anticonventional techniques. The books are companions, male–female variations on a common theme: how the slightest shock to our quotidian existence can knock everything askew, making further routine life impossible. *A Moment of True Feeling* and *The Left-Handed Woman* are stories of rebirth— painful and problematic because such new awareness makes each succeeding moment a matter to be reckoned with.

For most of their preceding lives, Gregor and Marianne have had little at all to reckon with. All has followed quite automatically, with Gregor's blank and meaningless embassy job and Marianne's colorless role of housewife largely taking care of themselves. Each has been a creature of routine, which is itself not boring as long as one proceeds in blissful ignorance. But as their respective stories begin, each is shocked into a recognition of how tenuous all of this has been. And after that, each advancing second of life becomes insipidly maddening, a unique crisis one is lucky to survive. Gregor Keuschnig's "moment of true feeling" comes upon awakening from a dream in which he has killed a woman. A Dostoevski hero would find this an occasion for psychological liberation, an excuse for making everything possible; Kafka, on the other hand, would keep life as it is, playing up the contrast between the familiarity of life and the utter transformation visited upon the character. Handke's position is fully different from each of these models: shaken out of his complacency, Gregor realizes that from now on he will be "only carrying on with his usual life for the sake of appearances" (p. 3). What was once a naive and innocent system running itself is now something to be questioned at every turn—for, after all, his uninhibited self has dreamed itself a murderer! "All at once," Handke writes, "he had ceased to belong." But still he must go on, in a life more personally tortuous than the philosophical struggles one might encounter in a Samuel Beckett novel:

> He tried to change, as an applicant for a job undertakes to change; but for fear of being found out he had to go on living exactly as before and, above all, remain exactly as he had been. Even to sit down as usual to a meal with other people was to dissemble; and if he suddenly began to talk so much about himself and his "past life," it was only to divert attention from himself. (p. 4)

In a dull life, in which everything had been assumed, now nothing is. Handke has found the prime materials for a novelist, because Gregor can no longer coast along—he must parse out every word, construct the grammar of each sentence, physically note each detail, and record with painstaking effort the most inconsequential matter. What for the

French new novelists was a technical exercise becomes for Gregor a necessary way of life: "Aloud he listed everything that was to be seen—that was his only way of perceiving" (p. 41).

In *The Left-Handed Woman,* Handke presents Marianne, aged thirty and the mother of an eight-year-old boy, whose life is similarly knocked out of adjustment by the chance assignment her son is working at: a copy-book exercise on a common theme, "my idea of a better life." His ideas are both infantile and instructive—temperate weather, no traffic, no studies, a world where "everything I don't know would disappear" (p. 4). Her husband is just returning from a long business trip, and in the face of his smug satisfaction with the way things are (he dotes on master-servant relationships and glories in the exercise of power), Marianne tells him to leave for good. Her *strange idea,* her *illumination,* is simply that there might be another way to live, a thought that her previously mundane routine could never allow. Gregor had been shocked by his dream of the impossible, which simply because he has dreamed it makes it a real aspect of his life. So, too, for Marianne; what had been unimaginable now forces itself upon her, just because she has thought of it. The imagination is powerfully creative, Handke insists. To think something is to will it conceptually, to recognize that it is possible; and to exercise the will in this systematically linguistic world is as good as making something happen. In any event, after such illuminations life can never be the same.

A flash of recognition—a sudden breakthrough to a truth that had rested there unnoticed, yet determinate all the same: how will life continue in the wake of such moments? What for a novelist of more conventional means would be a ponderously philosophical and internally dramatized answer becomes in Handke's hands a quintessentially novelistic matter. Gregor must continue his daily life, the affairs of which would constitute an unexceptional nineteenth-century bourgeois *roman.* Now, however, because of his sudden, disruptive insight and Handke's disposition to see all behavior in structurally linguistic terms, Gregor's life becomes a series of minute-to-minute adventures of life-and-death proportion. Gregor is alone within his drama, confessing his dream to no one. Marianne's act is more social, and people flock about her either to praise or to condemn—and also to discover correspondences in their own lives. Handke extends his novel by noting similar instances of shocking recognitions that change the lives in which they are lived. Marianne's employer tells this story, the structure of which mirrors Marianne's own:

> Not long ago, I broke with a girl I loved. The way it happened was so strange that I'd like to tell you about it. We were riding in a taxi at night. I had my arm around her, and we were both looking out the same side. Everything was fine. Oh yes, you have to know that she was very young—no more than twenty—and I was very fond of her. For the barest moment, just in passing, I saw a man on the sidewalk. I couldn't make out his features, the street was too dark. I only saw that he was rather young. And suddenly it flashed through my mind that the sight of that man outside would force the girl beside me to realize what an old wreck was holding her close, and that she must be filled with revulsion. The thought came as such a shock that I took my arm away. I saw her home, but at the door of her house I told her I never wanted to see her again. I bellowed at her. I said I was sick of her, it was all over between us, she should get out of my sight. And I walked off. I'm certain she still doesn't know why I left her. That young man on the sidewalk probably didn't mean a thing to her. I doubt if she even noticed him. (pp. 33–34)

As a novelist, Handke is careful to make every act in Marianne's life reflect this new quality of existence. A woman friend counsels fortitude and determination, while her widowed father comes to warn her about an impending life of loneliness. Her son, Stefan, and his fat friend are constant interruptions, persistent reminders of the sundered family life. She meets an actor who finds it hard to deliver lines, a shopgirl who is so lonely she gladly delivers change to the woman's home. Hired as a translator, she sets to work on a French memoir that seems the precise mirror of her own experience: *"Au pays de l'idéal: J'attends d'un homme qu'il m'aime pour ce que je suis et pour ce que de deviendrali. . . .* In the land of the ideal: I expect a man to love me for what I am and for what I shall become" (p. 35). Life is not easy; time hangs heavy on her hands now that every moment is self-willed and therefore self-conscious.

In *A Moment of True Feeling,* Marianne's loneliness is matched by Gregor's alienation. "To Keuschnig everything was equally far away and equally unreal. . . . It was as though his glance, before it could take anything in, had been blunted by an invisible barrier; it could reach nothing, and he felt no desire to reach anything" (p. 11). Life is easier, he learns, when things take care of themselves: "the bliss of a crowded timetable" (p. 24), days that arrange themselves in meaningless tasks. Under these new conditions, however, life is excruciatingly painful. He can only survive by thinking "word for word—as though thinking in words could protect him" (p. 50), counting his steps out loud as he walks, even thinking in complete sentences. Simply walking down the street and meeting fellow pedestrians is a curiously unreal chore: "He felt like a prisoner in Disneyland" (p. 15). What he seeks is a dreamless sleep, but his moment of true feeling (during uninhibited sleep) has taught him his waking life has been just that. And like suddenly discovering that he has been walking on thin ice (a metaphor to be used for the thematic title of Handke's play *The Ride Across Lake Constance)* or, like a cartoon character, that he has wandered out over the edge of a cliff, existence is now a tremulous affair—simply because he has to be aware of its every motion. "It was beyond him how he had found his way home every day," he must now reflect, "why he hadn't ever vanished on the way" (p. 68). Turning from a difficult scene with his daughter, "The mortar on the walls looked oozy; in another minute it would fall to the floor in cakes" (p. 97). Filmmaker Roman Polanski used the same device in *Repulsion* (1965) to visualize his heroine's discomposure and eventual psychosis. Such constant attention to a suddenly unstable world is exhausting. "When he considered how just this last hour had weighed on him," Gregor complains, "it was beyond him that he hadn't suffocated long ago" (p. 27). If one had to will each breath consciously, life might become too demanding to live, and this is just the feeling Handke has found appropriate for a life in which the comfortable, systematic routines have been removed. "It seemed to Keuschnig that this merciless, elemental time crawling along under the tall luminous sky had expelled all life from the world, that every manifestation of human beings had become a meaningless interlude" (p. 34). Worst of all, this monumental effort yields nothing proportionate to the effort, actually little of interest at all, leaving the protagonist to stare "with burning eyes into the same forever unchanging light—year in-year out with the same inexorability, predictability, moral tedium, and deadly exclusivity" (p. 62). This tedium is why life has become systematized in the first place; waking to a moment of true feeling may not be a blessing after all.

To survive, Gregor Keuschnig flirts with one solution, then embraces another. First he tries "to abolish everything," to commit an extroverted suicide by canceling the world itself. Then he tries various forms of escape: travel guides, diner's books for restaurants he will never visit, various escape routes, much as Handke's protagonist found in the America of *Short Letter, Long Farewell* (at one point a village in New England is fantasized for just this purpose). Gregor finally gets himself back into the currents of life by opening himself up to chance. Soon after his awakening he has noticed a sidewalk scribble: " '*Oh la bellie vie,*' and underneath, 'I am like you,' with a phone number. Whoever it was had BENT DOWN to write about the GOOD LIFE, he thought, and made a note of the phone number" (pp. 15–16). Here is a way to go on: a truly open-ended future, with a person he has never met, on the threshold of a new and better life. The novel concludes with Gregor resolving to keep his appointment with this unknown woman, and as he strides across the Place de l'Opera to his rendezvous the prose suddenly shifts from his own point of view to an anonymous narrator's: "On a balmy summer evening a man . . . strode resolutely toward the Café de la Paix" (p. 133). Is there any other way to live? For the first time since we have known him, Gregor is open to that possibility.

Gregor's decision to meet with the unknown woman is personally transformative. Finally in touch with the world, he presents an activity that can be observed, explaining the shift in narrative perspective that allows readers to observe him from outside himself. Before this point, he has been quite literally trapped within, for his grammar of relationship with the world had disintegrated with that one disturbing dream. By ceasing to belong, "for him a system had ceased to be possible" (p. 50), making it very hard to relate to persons, places, or things. The dream has awakened him and in this sense serves as "the first sign of life in me since God knows when," as Gregor admits to himself early in the novel. "It came to me because I'd been looking in the wrong direction, it wanted me to turn around. To wake me up and make me forget my somnambulistic certainties" (p. 25), which the routine practices of life create. But the destruction of one system, which by anesthetizing habit has become atrophied and is no longer keeping its user in touch with the world, is only the first step. Indeed, after establishing this process in *The Goalie's Anxiety, Short Letter,* and *A Sorrow Beyond Dreams,* Handke can in this novel accept it as the premise for necessary action: having been confronted with the obsolescence of his previous grammar of existence, the protagonist of *A Moment of True Feeling* must construct a new one from scratch, and his self-consciousness of this procedure provides the novel with a full and complex literary action.

In the world of Peter Handke's fiction, losing one's connection amid the reconcilation of concepts and reclamation of phenomena by which life otherwise goes on is more than a philosophical concept. Whereas an existential novelist might portray a character as alienated and leave it at that, Handke finds such a predicament to be only one part of a complex semiotic process from which true fiction can properly begin, not end. "*Alienation* is not even a technical term in post-structuralist thought," as Dean MacCannell and

Juliet Flower MacCannell explain in their study *The Time of the Sign: A Semiotic Interpretation of Modern Culture,* for when all we have is language there is nothing to be alienated from. It is no longer the world that is questioned but our systems of relationship to it:

> Today it is commonplace for individuals and groups, via words and deeds, to question *structure,* to question, that is, the validity of previously unchallenged associations, oppositions, and hierarchies. . . . Everything that was once thought to be a "fact," or a "self-evident truth," or a belief that could exist beyond question is now seen as a social expression or a *sign* . . . in the place of the subject/object split we are sending in the *sign,* a unification of subject and object or things and their meanings or values.[6]

Hence the genuine drama of Gregor's predicament: he must construct a new system of signification or, in other words, reinvent his world, much as a novelist does when contriving a fiction. On the one hand, Gregor envies simpler, mechanical orders, such as the one by which the police can operate, albeit reductively:

> He envied the policemen their faces. How beautiful they seemed to him in their self-assurance; beautiful because they had nothing to hide; beautiful in their unmarred extravertedness. In an emergency they would both know exactly what to do next, and what to do after that. As far as they were concerned, everything was tried and tested; nothing could go wrong because the ORDER of things had been set in advance. Every possibility had been gone over, every eventuality had been provided for. He saw them as pioneers, as Americans, from Grand Rapids, for instance—and such men could only be immortal! (p. 50)

The pioneer image recalls the self-apparent sign system Handke's protagonist found in the America of *Short Letter, Long Farewell.* But for Gregor Keuschnig as an Austrian living in Paris, there is no convenient New World to provide a system for his life. "He used to think that here in a foreign country, in a different language, the fits of terror he had had

6. Bloomington: Indiana University Press, 1982, pp. xi–xii.

all his life might take on a different meaning"; by living "less instinctively . . . he would no longer be so helplessly at their mercy as he had been in the land of his birth and childhood" (p. 87). But in Paris, as everywhere else, sign systems can decay into empty formulas as people go about their daily routines "as sure as death and taxes" (p. 61), leaving no real lives to live and no valid stories to tell. If anything happens *inevitably*, it might as well not happen at all: "Because everything had lost its validity," Gregor reflects, "he could imagine nothing" (p. 5). This is why his meeting with an unknown woman whose existence has been marked only by the most anonymous of chalk markings on a sidewalk, promising that life can be beautiful, is such a hopeful challenge. "Let's not arrange any signs," she urges Gregor when he phones her; "I'd like us just to recognize each other, I'll be there" (p. 17). Signs can be "gratuitously promising," such as the long, dark street named rue de l'Assomption that he passes when thinking of his promised meeting. "He hadn't wished for a sign, but now unintentionally he had EXPERIENCED one. Did he need it?" (p. 82). It is just this style of self-conscious examination that prevents significations from turning dead in his hands, which is what had happened before his moment of true feeling.

Gregor's narrative, like Handke's in *A Sorrow Beyond Dreams*, covers the full range of semiotic experience, from the objects he encounters to the linguistic form of their arrangements as signs. Placed from the start in the position of having to pretend to live as usual rather than proceeding securely and unselfconsciously within his daily routine, Gregor finds that he must make "a frantic effort to think in complete sentences" (p. 9). It is much easier simply to list things as objects, but that is not language, just as having to count one's steps aloud is hardly walking. Since he is functionally out of touch, "to Keuschnig everything was equally far away and unreal," as if "his glance, before it could take anything in, had been blunted by an invisible barrier; it could reach nothing, and he felt no desire to reach anything" (p. 11). Everything becomes an empty form, devoid of reality, as even a midday's lovemaking with his girlfriend in Montmartre is reduced to the purely formulaic: "the actions of laying-his-trousers-over-the-back-of-a-chair, of lying-down-in-bed-together, of inserting-the-penis-in-the-vagina" (p. 20). Objects are capitalized, experiences are hyphenated, and attitudes are italicized—all as a way of showing how language has become its own reality while life continues on, out of touch. Of himself, under these circumstances, there is nothing left "except the dead weight of an unreality at odds with the whole world" (p. 52). This is the weight of the world to which Handke himself will return two years later in his Paris journal of that title; for Gregor, everything in sight can become "a sign of death" (p. 19), and he longs "to find the beautiful strange land where death would no longer be a bodily presence" (p. 105). As Handke transcends the world's dead weight by writing—and by a living control of language transforming his own relation to existence—so Gregor vows to "reinvent himself" (p. 104).

His first order of business is to avoid the typicality that he finds revolting in others but to which he frequently falls victim himself, as when quoting the banalities of politicians to cover up his own anxiety. Instead, he must appreciate the mysteriousness of existence, in which something is "no longer a pointer to something else: it was a thing in its own right, beautiful or ugly in its own right, and ugly and beautiful in common with all other things"—such is the structure of an integral system of relationship with the world, far more than a simple case of alienation. In these circumstances, "particulars remote from one another" can nevertheless "vibrate with a kinship and harmony" for which he requires "no further memory or dream" (p. 121), a world truly unweighted by death, which in these terms can now be seen as an incorrectly subjective projection. Man-made objects can, when defined in terms of their use, be intimidating; but when Gregor himself is in control of the sign-making, as he is when noticing three randomly discarded objects lying on the ground before him, he is reminded that he has a future and can indeed change. As his old world dies around him (his wife has left him and his child has been lost, saved only by a friend who has been shadowing Gregor's displaced wanderings through town), he finds that by discarding the limitations of outmoded sign systems not of his own making he can be perceptually reborn.

Is Gregor Keuschnig a mystic, as Handke's protagonist in *Short Letter* felt himself becoming when swept up by nature's own heartbeat? In *The Left-Handed Woman,* this charge is leveled against Marianne soon after he decision to break from married life, as if she is a "private mystic" whom "a bit of electroshock would straighten . . . out" (p. 22). Though *mysticism* can be a term of alienation when viewed from the perspective of others, Handke has been careful in his novels to employ it as a strategy not against society but as a tactic to remove oneself from the automatism of dead significations: Gregor at the end of his novel and Marianne at the start of hers are less antisocial than they are determinedly antisystematic. "Don't be alone too much," Marianne is cautioned early on: "It could be the death of you" (p. 23). What her friend implies is that by removing herself from the grammar of relationships she will lose her place in the world. What Handke's method shows is just the opposite: to be truly alive, a person cannot accept other people's significations, especially when those labels are claimed as absolute (as Marianne's friends try to tell her what she is like). Such comments are insults, she decides, which is one of her first steps toward creating her own viable world.

The only thing wrong with systems, Handke's fiction argues, is that they can become vehicles for the imposition of one person's ideas of order upon another. Marianne's friend Franziska, for example, can champion woman's independence as an issue, but only when it is accommodated within the systematics of group activity—one formulation is simply replaced by another. "Please come to our group meeting tomorrow night," she urges Marianne, whose actual freedom shocks her own sense of conformity within rebellion: "We need someone who's slightly nuts" (p. 27). In the same breath, she reveals her stereotypical prejudice by cautioning Marianne against solitary drinking, just as her husband, Bruno, will later return to make snide comments about their child's symptoms of alienation. "These are indications," he menacingly suggests (p. 39), as a prelude to his vicious condemnation of what he sees as her future:

> So here you are, living the good life, alone with *your* son, in a nice warm house with a garden and garage and good fresh air! Let's see, how old are you? You'll soon have folds in your neck and hairs growing out of your moles. Little spindly legs with a potato sack on top of them. You'll get older and older, you'll say you don't mind, and one day you'll hang yourself. You'll stink in your grave as uncouthly as you've lived. And how do you pass the time in the meanwhile? You probably sit around biting you nails. Right? (p. 49)

Bruno's paragraph reads like the descriptions of a conventionally realistic novelist, the style of writer who believes that the credibility of individual lives is measured by how accurately they conform with the universally accepted formulas of the character's social context. It is the tyranny of such formulations, which are made to seem natural rather than the cultural devices they really are, that both Handke as creator and Marianne as his character set themselves against. As the final test, Marianne's father comes to visit her with a similarly deterministic warning, right out of naturalistic fiction. "I believe that at some time I began to live in the wrong direction" (p. 59), he tells his daughter, and since then time has hung heavy on his hands. "You'll end up the same as me, Marianne," he cautions. "And with this observation my mission here is fulfilled" (pp. 60–61).

Marianne's intentions are just the opposite. Time has hung very heavy on her own hands because she had let herself become a factor in her husband's system of dominance. He has been perfectly comfortable in a world that makes him king, admiring what he calls "the mature beauty of the feudal master-servant relationship" (p. 10) and, even after being separated from his family, anxious to show his son his carefully planned strategies for intimidating the people he must deal with in his office. In retrospect, his lordly behavior at the novel's beginning seems ludicrous once Marianne has set off on her own: her act of independence reveals just how his systematizing of existence depends upon other people's domination. "Tonight I feel the need of being served like this!" he proclaims on his first evening home from the long business trip, oblivious to the needs his wife and son may have felt in his absence: "How sheltered one feels! A taste of eternity!" (p 10). He insists on dining out and then on grandly ordering a night's room at the hotel, exclaiming, "My wife and I want to sleep together right away." Like the hero in the master-servant novel he has read on the flight home, Bruno revels in such systematic control of the world, which he praises as a literary critic: "To be waited on in this proud, respectful way, if only for a brief moment at tea, reconciles him [the novel's hero] not only with himself but also, in some strange way, with the whole human race" (p. 11). Living this way, Bruno can boast of a magic power that he feels is making all his wishes come true. "And I need you" (p. 12), he tells his wife. But Marianne's illumination is into the syntax of this relationship, which is definitely one way: his *need* of her is functioning as a transitive verb, making her an object acted upon to establish Bruno's active subjecthood. To relate comfortably with the world, he must first dominate her, with no thought of her desire to exist as a subject herself.

Bruno's structure of existence is much easier than the challenge faced by Marianne, as long as others cooperate in their subservience. But once Marianne takes herself out of it, his system collapses like a house of cards, and he spends the balance of the novel wandering through the wreckage of his once grand synthesis, pathetically conspiring to put it back in order. Part of Marianne's problem is to fend him off, just as she must resist the critical judgments tendered by her friends who are suspicious of behavior so different from their own. She therefore resists strong personalities, the type of characters who in a novel set the tone for action and color their surroundings, including other characters. As she tells Franziska, any other man she might take up with could not be someone who advertises his identity—as Bruno did—as a point of control. She longs for a friend ("body and soul," Franziska prompts her), but "I don't want to know who he is. Even if I were always with him, I wouldn't want to know him." If anything, she would prefer someone clumsy, "a regular butterfingers" (p. 54), for anyone in deft control of the world necessarily must work his determinations on other people. Her own independence, she insists, is purely anarchic: "The only political action I could understand would be to run amok" (p. 55). She would thus reject the order of programmatic disorder lest her revolution contradict itself and make her once again a prisoner of extrinsic form.

Yet there is a terrible loneliness in living apart from other peoples' systems, almost to the point that Marianne fears she will not exist. As Franziska comments during the novel's penultimate scene, a party attended by a group of disconnected characters, "Loneliness is a source of loathsome ice-cold suffering, the suffering of unreality. At such times we need people to teach us that we're not really so far gone" (p. 80). Hence, Handke as author puts his novel to the test by assembling everyone who has taken part in the action individually to see if any workable relationships are possible—in other words, to see if a world can be made from the components that have distinguished themselves by their demand for integral existence. As in Handke's play *The Ride Across Lake Constance,* the struggle is for each character to express himself or herself without defining that self by someone else's role. It is a difficult challenge, for social groups are defined by their relationships, just as language consists of structured differences (or comparisons). But by having the characters honestly face each other at the end, Handke unmasks the totally conventional nature of these relationships, and what was once a determining absolute no longer boasts the power to control identities.

First to disappear is the master-servant relationship, as the publisher's chauffeur is invited in to join the party. In similar manner, Franziska discards her role as teacher to deal personally with the salesgirl, who has herself demanded to be known for something other than her job. Then Bruno's lingering sense of sexual dominance is put to rest in his confrontation with the diffident actor who has been courting Marianne. Originally introduced as one who is "not shameless enough for an actor," a person who never risks his own self and as a result is "always posing" (p. 63), he can now face up to Bruno's attempt to stereotype him as "the boyfriend" and as "the type that drives an ancient small car with a lot of political pornography magazines lying around on the back seat" (p. 78). He can assert the individuality he has wished to share with Marianne, without wishing to take back everything the moment he says it. She asks of him only one thing: "Please don't put me in any of your plans" (p. 83). If he is to love her, it must be for what she is as herself, not for what she can be for him. To be recognized as an individual and not as a functional part of someone else's system is her demand, just as the lyrics of the song she plays over and over express; "The Left-Handed Woman" can be apart from the crowds of office workers and subway riders only when the marks of her individuality are given chance for expression:

> The telephone receiver is facing the wrong way,
> The pencil lies to the left of the writing pad,
> The teacup next to it has its handle on the
> Left,
> The apple beside it has been peeled the wrong way
> (but not completely),
> The curtains have been thrown open from the left
> And the key to the street door is in the left
> Coat pocket.
> Left-handed woman, you've given yourself away!
> Or did you mean to give me a sign?
> I want to see you in a foreign continent,
> For there at last I will see you alone among others,
> And among a thousand others you will see me,
> And at last we shall go to meet each other.
>
> (p. 68)

The way for characters to relate, she has learned, is to meet within their selves—as with the meeting at the Café de la Paix that concludes *A Moment of True Feeling*, extrinsic sign systems must not be allowed to predict future events. Only from such a fresh position can valid systems of relationships be formed so that individual essences can determine the structure of existence and not the other way around.

Marianne's conclusion in *The Left-Handed Woman* is not as dramatic as Gregor's transformation at the end of *A Moment of True Feeling,* but it is no less significant. Her impromptu party among all the characters previously named in the novel ends with her resolution to remain herself: "Standing at the hall mirror, she brushed her hair. She looked into her eyes and said, 'You haven't given yourself away. And no one will ever humiliate you again' " (p. 87). She then does something she hasn't done before; she picks up a note pad and sketches the things around her, "each object in every detail." She goes on living, but now in control of her surroundings rather than allowing them to control her, yet she does not steal from them their individuality, either. The novel ends with a quotation from Goethe, about how "even in desperate situations where everything hangs in the balance, one goes on living as though nothing were wrong." But for his film version of *The Left-Handed Woman* (which he scripted and directed), Handke chose a more activist message, superimposing the following words across the closing scene of the Metro entrance that leads from the woman's claustrophobic suburb to the city world beyond: "Have you noticed? There's only room for those who make room for themselves."[7] What Marianne learns as a person parallels what Handke has demonstrated for creating full characters within the axioms of postmodern writing: that a full life of fiction is the best antidote to the death of the novel.

7. Written and directed by Peter Handke in 1978 for Road Movies Filmproduktion, Munich.

IV. The New Sensibility

> As long as I am still alone, I am still alone.
> As long as I am among acquaintances, I am still an acquaintance.
> But as soon as I am among strangers—
>
> —"Changes during the Course of the Day"

Recent German literature has experienced a fundamental transformation from espoused goals of political enlightenment, predominant in the radical 1960s, to a recourse to inwardness and subjectivity—hence the intensified sensibility so apparent in the writing of the 1970s and early 1980s. The literature of the sixties, witness to a new and militant student movement, saw its goal in the politicization of a passively pliant populace suffocated by alienation and made to be minor cogs in a commodity-producing machinery that reified social and personal relationships to marketable values. The purveyors of this new enlightenment, largely Marxist by conviction and pupils of the critical theorists Ardono, Bloch, Marcuse, and Horkheimer, stressed intellectual liberation as a force toward social change—a profoundly rational process that affirmed the traditional interpretive systems of science, scholarship, and philosophy as methods comprehending and subverting the existing social order. Young activists understood their task to be the rational negation of the rampant irrationalism inherent in the system.

The collapse of the student movement in the late 1960s—signaled by the failure in 1968 of the student and worker revolt in France, the end of the Vietnam war several years later (along with its quieting effect in the United States), and increasing political repression in West Germany—brought about a host of subtle changes in the younger generation of middle-class intellectuals. As in the United States, resistance began to subside and to assume new forms of expression. Political action was turned inward and became the conspicuous introspection typical of the numerous "alternative" movements that grew in the seventies and today flourish in West Germany's cities and countryside, spawning the Green movement that gained national strength and international recognition with its election to the *Bundestag* in March 1983. The alternative movements have softened their once universal demand for revolutionary action and have redirected their attention to more modestly specific goals, including feminism, environmental issues, and the antinuclear peace movement.

If alienation and commodification could not be overcome in the political arena—and this was the thrust of the largely documentary-style literature that dominated the 1960s—then they had to be resisted by a reemphasized subjectivity in groups and individuals dedicated to reexamining and renewing their contacts to self and nature in the quest for private transformation. The political struggle had failed, and rather than seek the reason for this failure in the prevailing order, many German intellectuals sought reasons in themselves, in self-perceived inadequacy. Thus, introspection as a form of self-doubt began to supplant militant political action; subjectivity gained ascendency over critical theory. Instead of following Marx's dictum that the goal of philosophy was not to comprehend the world but to change it, writers of the 1970s such as Peter Handke, Nicolas Born, Jürgen Theobaldy, Botho Strauss, and Peter Schneider turned their quests inward, attempting to stake out epistemological conditions of knowledge and perception untainted by established norms. This is not to say that these writers reject political activism as an attempt to change the world; rather, they try to establish what Christa Wolf has termed "subjective authenticity":[1] their reality as perceiving and knowing subjects freed from the burden of the

1. Christa Wolf, "Subjektive Authentizität und gesellschaftliche Wahrheit: Erin Gespräch mit Christa Wolf," Auskünfte. Werkstattgespräche mit *DDR-Autoren* (Berlin and Weimar: Aufbau, 1976), pp. 492–93.

systems of domination that control the functional world and threaten the last vestiges of individual identity, of "self" and "I" as uniquely existing phenomena.

The literature of new subjectivity is intensely individualistic. It views the public sphere as a realm imbued with and dominated by forces beyond individual control—in short, as a world of unfreedom. Human existence has been stripped of its decisive aspect of subjectivity; that is, its primal self-identity as the knowing and creative subject of human history is repressed. Instead, through this absorption of self into a world of reified objects, people have become objects of alienated social and historical forces beyond their control. Human existence has become what Marcuse described as a condition of "streamlined servitude."[2] If the public sphere has become impenetrable to rational and active cognition, and if even language, that vital mediator between subjective individuality and the outerworld, has been rendered suspect by its use as an instrument of political and economic manipulation, then there remains but one alternative: retreat into an innerworld to discover and actualize an authentic and purely individual "I." This new subjectivity then can set out on an intellectual journey to reconquer a world of objects untainted by preexistent systems of perception and to impose on these objects one's own individuality—to recreate them as purely concrete knowledge. This is the quest undertaken by many of the writers of the New Sensibility who, in refusing to affirm the existing order of things, invoke the subversive power of negativity residing in their art. In doing so, they attempt to construct visible antagonisms between individuals and the existing social order by reappropriating the world and displaying this newly created universe of fiction as personally secured knowledge imbued with subjectivity. The fiction of New Sensibility stands as a counterweight to the prevailing order; its steadfast refusal to affirm the world as it is militates as an impetus toward change.

The renewed subjectivity of the New Sensibility does not

2. Herbert Marcuse, *Studies in Critical Philosophy* (Boston: Beacon Press, 1972), p. 214.

necessarily lead, as some critics have charged, to incontrovertable solipsism, for subjectively secured knowledge has an objective component guaranteed by the intersubjective nature of human consciousness. Kant's epistemological critique, after all, assumes the outerworld to consist of chaotic raw material that is appropriated and ordered as knowledge by the imposition of the categories inherent in human consciousness—those of time and space, for instance—upon the world, thus reconstituting reality in a supremely creative way. In an article on Peter Handke, Peter Pütz emphasizes this aspect of the new-subjective literature: "Authors of the present see themselves compelled to first of all explore in quasi-transcendental literary reflection the preconditions of the possibility of perception and representation. This expedition leads, as with Descartes, undeniably into the realm of subjectivity, which is not identical to the private solus ipse."[3] Moreover, the charges of excessive privateness and obscurity leveled against new-subjective literature are nullified by the striking popularity of writers such as Strauss, Born, and Handke.

The largely autobiographical literature of New Sensibility represents the attempt to communicate this process and to transfer it to the reader by subverting and estranging his experience of nature and society. New-subjective fiction endeavors to "explode the pre-established structure of meaning and, becoming an 'absolute object' itself, designate an intolerable, self-defeating universe—a discontinuum."[4]

Hans-Gerhard Winter has constructed a set of six criteria to describe and define the literature of the New Sensibility:

> 1) This literature constructs its world "from the figural perspective. . . . The environment only becomes visible in that the main character perceives it";
> 2) "innerworld and outerworld merge";

3. Peter Pütz, *Kritisches Lexikon zur deutschsprachigen Gegenwarsliteratur*, ed. Heinz Ludwig Arnold (Munich: Edition text und kritik, 1978), p. 8 of Handke entry.

4. Herbert Marcuse, *One-Dimensional Man* (Boston: Beacon Press, 1964), p. 69.

3)"with the elimination of the outerworld, the main character appears in complete self-referentiality";
4) new-subjective literature "thematizes the identity problem";
5) these works do not limit themselves to "recording phenomena; they also demonstrate in a limited way means of overcoming this condition" of self-referentiality;
6) open conclusions characterize new-subjective writing: "It contains the demand upon the reader to think out the story and also to continue to question himself."[5]

It quickly becomes evident that much of Handke's literature fits into Winter's categories. From *The Goalie's Anxiety at the Penalty Kick* through *Short Letter, Long Farewell* and *A Sorrow Beyond Dreams* to *A Moment of True Feeling* and *The Left-Handed Woman,* Handke's fiction has emphasized the subjective and autobiographical aspects of narration even before they were in fashion. His characters are in a constant quest for identity with themselves and the world. This should come as no surprise to readers of Handke's essay "I Am an Ivory Tower Dweller"; even in 1964 Handke expressed the conviction that for him literature "is a means to become, if not clear, then at least clearer about myself. It has helped me to recognize that I existed, that I was in the world" (p. 19). Literature, he continues, has given him a means to destroy all apparently valid systems of viewing the world. "And because I have recognized that I could change myself through literature, that I could, through literature, live more consciously. I am also convinced that, through my literature, I can change others" (p. 20). For Handke, literature has only one purpose, "to become aware and to make others aware: more sensitive, more perceptive . . . so that I and others can exist more precisely, more sensitively, so that I can communicate better with myself and better deal with others" (p. 26).

With the publication of *The Weight of a World* (1977, as yet untranslated), however, Handke at once radicalized and

5. "Von der Dokumentarliteratur zur 'neuen Subjektivität': Amnerkungen zur westdeutschen Literatur der siebziger Jahre," *Seminar* 17 (1981): 69.

expanded new-subjectivity tendencies already present in his thought and writing. In this most unusual journal, encompassing the period of his life in Paris from November 1975 to March 1977, and dedicated to "those it concerns," writing becomes the process of self-reduction to an actively perceiving "I" that constitutes both itself and the outerworld by perceiving, recording, and thus preserving objects and events as pure knowledge imbued with subjectivity—and thus saved from the process of reification into the estranged network of hostile signification systems confronting individuals in the public sphere. But *The Weight of the World* also adds a new dimension to Handke's literature. For the first time, subjective perception and the literary representation of that perception is deemed insufficient as a process in itself. *The Weight of the World* thus signals a new period in Handke's writing, marked by his desire to go beyond subversion and deconstruction of preexisting systems toward constructing generally valid meaning.

Outerworld segments appropriated by consciousness must, to gain compelling force for others, be tied into a greater system of signification. This system, Handke now recognizes, is myth as a sense-giving link between individuals and a greater sociocultural whole. If there is to be meaning in people's lives, Handke's journal indicates, it must be created by the poet who can penetrate the "idiocy of language" (a phrase that Handke uses often) and create an exemplary new world containing the impetus to create new myths to replace the exhausted ones of Western culture and so relink alienated individuals with their roots in nature. Nature, myth, and history have thus become the themes of Handke's literature of the late 1970s and early 1980s. As a result, one of the first German-language authors to delve into himself in search of subjective authenticity demonstrates a potential exit from the introspective stance of the New Sensibility—the quest of the poet-redeemer, purified through the process of coming to self, for universally valid myth in nature and culture—"Time and time again the necessity as a writer to invent myths, to find them: myths which have nothing to do with the old myths of western culture; as if I needed new myths, innocent ones acquired from my daily life with which I can begin myself again" (p. 181).

The Weight of the World represents Handke's most radical attempt to come to grips with the world as perception and with the reflection of this perceived world as language. As with *A Sorrow Beyond Dreams,* the author once again turns to family history to see whether his newly achieved fictional techniques can bear the test of life. But Handke avoids the traditional diary form in favor of a protocol-like registering of unsorted and purposeless perceptions, all arranged in generally brief entries consisting of sentences and fragments. Such a seemingly peculiar undertaking is in line with the positivistic method developed by the Vienna Circle philosophers Rudolf Carnap and Ludwig Wittgenstein, who insisted that scientific knowledge, to maintain its empirical base and thus remain verifiable, must be reducible to immediate sense perceptions. Wittgenstein and the Vienna Circle mistrusted the abstractions of modern intellectual constructs, and the implicit bias of positivism toward the minimal is an attempt to extract the truly scientific from the metaphysical underpinnings of knowledge. Handke's *Weight of the World* proceeds in a similar vein, attempting to liberate from the ideologically perverted body of language the substratum of truth that resides in raw perception, clothed only in minimal language form. Thus Handke chooses a nonsequential, noncausal diary as his vehicle, discarding the traditional form of a personal diary in favor of a deliberately unsystematic recording of unordered perceptions. Most writing of any sort presumes a framework in which perceptions are ordered by a central intelligence that guides the process of selection, sorting, and ultimate presentation. But this very process is the crux of the problem for Handke, for in it resides the danger that this world, instead of being perceived with absolute neutrality, will be filtered through a shaping consciousness and thus limited by ideology and misdirected by rhetoric.

Handke therefore sets himself the task of mechanically registering his sense perceptions in the form of diary entries with no intended connections. Each stands alone as an experiential monad naturally sealed off against the others. Hence, Handke's journal is not much of a find for biographers, for although some personal details work their way in, such as the death of a friend or a stay in the hospital, the only pattern is that of coincidence—no meanings are allowed to accumulate.

In the introduction, Handke points out that he had first intended to use these notes as the plan for a story or a silent play. Thus, he initially translated his daily observations into the system for which they were needed. This concept of utility consequently guided a process of selection in which useful perceptions were recorded for later use, while others that did not fit were forgotten. But soon the intense concentration needed to record such minute impressions made Handke aware of all he was neglecting. Hence, he began noting, as he says, "even events of consciousness which could not be used for the project" (p. 5). As a result, the original plan was scrapped and Handke began recording even insignificant perceptions, all of which gave him a sense of liberation from traditional literary genres and at the same time a freedom of possibility he had not known: writing without purpose. In order to achieve his goal, Handke practiced reacting with language to everything that happened. Each perception thus became an event clothed in words: "No matter what I experienced, this 'moment of language' appeared to me universal and free of all privateness" (p. 6).

The change from observation guided by a clear concept of selection and purpose to randomly recorded perceptions is clearly marked in the journal entry for 6 March 1976, in which Handke expresses a new awareness: everything that has happened to him in the past has melted together into an amorphous mass no longer accessible to language nor expressible in images. If this dissolution of experience is to be overcome, Handke's writing must transform the mass "into something substantially different so that writing may be an awakening of these thousands and thousands of amorphously encapsulated forms" (p. 31). Even apparently insignificant perceptions must be recorded to rescue them from oblivion. A few examples illustrate Handke's technique:

> The child's ear in the shadow under her hair. (p. 35)
>
> The dead cars in front of the windows at night. (p. 57)
>
> Certainty that, when I am really friendly, nothing can go wrong. (p. 65)
>
> The skin still sticky in the places where the electrodes were fastened. (p. 95)
>
> We said so much to each other so quickly that we just sat there and made swallowing sounds. (p. 179)
>
> When in the course of the day language arises, becomes, comes to consciousness, is found: Revitalization of dead nature. (p. 310)
>
> How to achieve monumentality in self-expression that the great writers have attained? By periodically living without restraint. (p. 205)
>
> Deep within myself, I warmed myself, untouchable by the functional world. (p. 324)
>
> Dream that I had died: The feeling of death was a presentiment of the coldness of the morgue. (p. 218)

These examples show the random character of Handke's observations. Although most of the notations have no common theme, they are permeated with a sense of anxiety, a fear of death. A disdain for time and history, characteristic of much twentieth-century Austrian literature—Hermann Broch and Robert Musil are good examples—shows itself in the character of many of the entries: a desire to overcome time and history and find new meaning in myth. Handke's intention is, after all, to save experience from dissolution into an indeterminate mass. Therefore, he must mold each experience, each perception, to lift it out of the transitory flow of time without perverting it by imposing ideology or rhetoric. "The experience of history, that means for me: to liberate myself from it, to be liberated from it" (p. 138).

We have seen that Handke understands reality as a self-created structure—a false construct that, permeating consciousness and language, contains within it the system of domination that dictates relationship within a given society. Like the neopositivist philosophers of the Vienna Circle who, in order to free scientific thought from its metaphysical limits, attempted to reduce all valid knowledge to immediate experience, Handke sets out to reexperience, to reperceive the world directly by circumventing the usual epistemological process that calls for fitting each perception into a hierarchy of consciousness, thus debasing pure experience itself: "Words like 'reality' are euphemisms; using them, even to criticize them ('the dictate of reality'), would mean giving this obscure 'reality' an advantage it does not deserve" (p. 192).

As Handke learned from his apprenticeship in the postmodern aesthetic, literature must reflect critically upon the language it uses; this way language may be freed from its implicitly purveyed sense that there is a prior interconnectedness of things, a preexistent meaning in the world that justifies certain acts. Handke sees his writing as "searching out the places not yet occupied by meaning" (p. 276), and by doing this he hopes to supplant the didactic literature of Brecht with a more personal and direct style. But what is radically new here is Handke's turn from direct experience as a dissembling of corrupt reality (which is nothing more than an empty construct) to personal perception in search of myth that might provide life with meaning: "Deconstruct naturalist forms until didactic, demonstrative ones appear (Brecht); deconstruct the didactic forms until mythical ones appear (my writing)" (p. 321).

As in the works that followed the publication of *The Weight of the World*, which share an obsession with aesthetic inwardness, Handke's diaristic entries delve into the history of art and literature in quest of aesthetic forms, artistic beauty, myth, and nature. The journal is strewn with quotes from Handke's readings in the sixteen-month period covered: Goethe, Hesse, Novalis, and Kafka, to name a few, provide the author with insights that might be transformed into knowledge and expression. This quest is also one for literary language, for lasting formulations that might transcend the corrupt expression of everyday life: "sometimes the feeling that all the advertising slogans and the inescapable headlines of the scandal sheets would one day literally beat me to death" (p. 65). Reading is a search for self-expression and self-knowledge as well as a means to deconstruct exhausted formulations and jargon. "For each one of my sentences, the psychoanalyst employed a code which was, however, only part of another preformulated language system: The task would be to desystematize all preformulated language systems; not to find new codes, but rather to decodify those which already exist" (pp. 61–62).

Thus, *The Weight of the World* marks a turning point in Handke's writing, a change that becomes even more evident in his recent novels: the search for new forms of self-expression has led to a quest for myth as the core of meaning. Handke's early prose proceeded from a fundamental critique of language as a social institution linking the individual as knowing and perceiving subject with an estranged world of people and objects. The material world, Handke would have argued, is not accessible to knowledge. As part of a reflective system, language acquisition is an appropriation of the outerworld in symbolic form. Its objects, after all, cannot be seized physically and put within consciousness. But in a rapidly changing world these symbols, once established, become petrified; they continue to exist in a fixed form, even though the world they represent is in flux. Thus they provide an illusion of mastery—mastery of a world that no longer exists. Hence, language becomes an empty form, no longer able to represent and express. The break of this link to the outerworld makes that world look strangely unfocused and unknowable.

Handke's mature prose has its foundation in the consciousness of this widening break; its emotional core is the feeling of forlornness and estrangement. But instead of reverting to the language study of his earlier works, Handke now signals a retreat to a new subjectivity that leads to a critique of consciousness instead. It is here that the perceiving epistemological core, the "I," resides. Handke's version of the New Sensibility establishes the singularity of his consciousness. In this inchoate state he can proceed to reexperience and reconquer the object world as something concrete and coherent.

Handke's recent books are characterized by a powerful yearning for redemption, for a healing of the schism between "I" and the outerworld. *Slow Journey Home* (1979, as yet untranslated), a book in style and concept quite unusual by the standards of the author's earlier prose, begins with a ponderous sentence: "Sorger had survived several people who had been near to him and no longer experienced desire, but often a selfless joy in existing and, at the same time, an animal-like craving for salvation which pressed heavily upon his eyelids" (p. 9). Sorger's suffering stems from his feelings of desperation, fear, and uncertainty inherent in the experience of the factual world's singularity and unconnectedness, especially when unleashed and uncontrolled by the traditional signification systems of myth and symbol. The world as appearance has no inherent intersubjective meaning. It needs, as Sorger sees it, the form-giving effort of human subjectivity to provide it—as myth—with meaning.

Sorger, a geologist working in the far north of Alaska, is overwhelmed by the desire to create a new science that will be capable of reconstituting the world as objective knowledge permeated with pure subjectivity. Sorger the scientist cannot continue trying to discover the world; he knows he must reinvent it by projecting his own subjectivity while at the same time discovering universal categories that could act as guidelines. For the categories underlying his investigation, Sorger, like Kant before him, relies on space, time, form, and what he calls "The Law."

A chapter is devoted to each of these categories, which mark the stations along Sorger's odyssey from Alaska ("The Forms of Prehistory") to California ("Prohibition of Space") and, finally, via Colorado and New York, home ("The Law")—a journey Sorger never completes. Like many Austrian writers, Handke-Sorger is obsessed with a fear of time and history, as these represent the fleeting, transitory aspects of life. Thus Sorger takes refuge in space and form, both of which have their existence outside the temporal realm. Sorger, the metaphysical geologist permeated by forlorness, seeks salvation in form and space as shelters against the onslaught of time. By experiencing and defining the spatial form of his area, a remote Indian village, he makes his immediate surroundings into his own personal space. In conquering space and form, he reconquers the spatial form of his own past and can hope to fit such individually gained units of conquered reality together in a vast and knowable entity that, like a great dome, might "encompass heaven and earth as a private sanctuary which opens itself to others as well" (p. 15). Sorger's science thus becomes a new mystic religion that creates myths by imposing universal subjectivity upon nature. Sorger adds, "And I would like to impart reason to the landscape and sadness to heaven" (pp. 34–35).

But when leaving Alaska to return to his university in California ("Prohibition of Space"), Sorger sees his timeless world of harmony and progress fall apart. He reminds himself that his pastoral idyll had neglected the historical dimensions of his being, and now he sees himself as the "progeny of evil-doers," as the son of "the genocidal murderers of this century" (p. 99). In a further experience, Sorger becomes aware that his harmonious relationship with nature had excluded people. His world of form and space shatters like a broken crystal sphere: "Today a power abandoned me, and I lost my special sense for the forms of the earth. From one moment to the next my spaces were no longer capable of signification, no longer worthy of signification" (p. 140).

This recognition leads Sorger to a near-breakdown; he aimlessly wanders around the countryside near his home, on the verge of collapse. But just at this moment his neighbor, a good friend whose close and devoted family life provides an example, drives by and saves Sorger from himself. Here, the self-sufficient and deeply introverted Sorger begins to sense the need for others, for human ties. Form and space are themselves inadequate guidelines for life.

Now alienation assumes a particularly human dimension. Sorger discovers that redemption cannot be achieved in space and form alone, but rather in the humanizing nature of culture: "Today I remembered a kind of redemption. No God came to mind, but rather culture. I have no culture" (p. 141). As a perpetual outsider, Sorger's feeling of loneliness can only be overcome by a critically reflected affirmation of the world as it is coupled with a renewed interest in people and in the need to change that world for people: "I need the reassurance that I am myself and, at the same time, responsible for others. Thus I raise claim to the world and this century—for it is my world and my century" (p. 141).

Sorger's inwardness of form and space, now disrupted, gives way to a new need to establish intense relationships with people and their endeavors. These he subsumes under the concept of culture, which as Sorger sees it is the net sum of human activity. And it is as such a reaffirmation of his own time—the very present that he had so vociferously rejected while in Alaska. Thus his thoughts change from personal salvation to the redemption of the world. As if to illustrate this change, Sorger meets a fellow Austrian in New York, a man in dire need of help and understanding. He spends the night counseling this man, who is able to return home the next day (perhaps vicariously for Sorger?) to face his family and work.

In this last section of *Slow Journey Home*, Sorger's quest turns to an "invented world which will detach itself . . . from the real world" (p. 155). This new world must be a construct of myth valid for all people in his culture. Consequently, Sorger seeks a universally binding personal code ("The Law"), which will guide him in his life and work. Part of this experience is reaffirming history as a positive force as well as a form whose progress he, as well as others, can act upon. Immortality, says Sorger, can be reached in history as part of being through the ages—hence his personal law, which he is now finally able to articulate: "I declare myself responsible for my future. I yearn for eternal reason and no longer want to be alone. So be it" (p. 169). Sorger's view of nature includes himself as an active human viewer who, by his act of cognition, constitutes the forms of nature and makes nature a human realm. Here history assumes a messianic face: salvation may be achieved in the self-fulfillment of history, for "Sorger believed that the history of humanity would soon be completed, in harmony, without horror. Yes, there was salvation (wasn't there?)" (p. 199). This messianic view lets Sorger perceive himself as reborn, and he begins his journey to Europe with the hope that his life has truly begun anew.

Slow Journey Home has been attacked by European critics as arrogant, presumptuous, and obscure. More tellingly, a French review of the 1982 translation *(Lent Retour)* was titled "Peter Handke: The Goalie is Tired."[6] A German commentator accused Handke of presuming to be "the new messiah of nature,"[7] as if his solution were no more than trite escapism. Yet Handke's novel is more readable than his early prose and is more accessible than any of his plays. It revels in a sense of pleasure from pure narration, with complexly subordinate constructions and minute detail. Its selection of vocabulary and narrative style betrays a refashioning of eighteenth- and nineteenth-century modes—we know that Goethe, Keller, and Stifter guided Handke's artistic development. These features in turn reveal a renewed interest in more simply human concerns for which nature is only the most apparent metaphor. *Slow Journey Home,* Handke has emphasized, represents the attempt to negate the fragmentary character of modern experience by creating harmony and beauty to serve as a counterweight to the existing world's banality. The novel, which he calls an "epic poem," is an "attempt to reach a world harmony and at the same time to reach a universality for myself as someone who writes. . . . I have the feeling that for centuries this has not been tried: To capture this harmony with language, and to

6. André Clavel, "Le Dernier Peter Handke: Le gardien de but est fatigué," *Les Nouvelles Littéraires,* 5–12 May 1982, p. 52.

7. Urs Jenny, "Ein Messias der Natur," *Der Spiegel* 26 (20 May 1982), p. 247.

pass it on contagiously."[8] But beauty and harmony, once created, become hermetically enveloped entities that "come into conflict with the history of my ancestors, which is also in me." Unlike the hermetic self-apparency of his earlier work, Handke's recent writing has begun to emphasize "problems with home, with language, with family, with history, with nature."[9] These are the themes that continue to be important in the remaining volumes of the homecoming tetralogy, especially in the concluding book, *Through the Villages,* in which questions of home and family take a central role.

June Schlueter reports that in an earlier version of the homecoming manuscript the main character, called Quitt (suggesting "to quit" or "to give up"), fails in his quest, finally choosing suicide as the only way out of his conflict. The Sorger of the published novel solves this deadly contradiction by finding solace in friendship and family—by recognizing that personal redemption lies in helping others. This is a theme that Handke would continue developing in the remaining volumes of his homecoming cycle. His progress has always been toward the most personally human applications of postmodern aesthetics, and his recent work bears the test of intimacy with the central philosophical problems of our age.

In his newest fiction, Handke seems more ready to accept the linguistic state of affairs, devoting his efforts toward more active work with other forms of perception and communication by which life proceeds. *The Lesson of Sainte Victoire* (1980, as yet untranslated) appears to be a book about Paul Cézanne, in particular the painter's later work; the Sainte Victoire of the title refers to a mountain range in Provence where Cézanne found his most challenging subjects, and it is Handke's metaphor for how, against the most severe aesthetic tests, life goes on. But a book like this is hard to classify. *The Lesson of Sainte Victoire* is not fiction, at

8. June Schlueter, *The Plays and Novels of Peter Handke* (Pittsburgh: University of Pittsburgh Press, 1981), p. 176.
9. Ibid., p. 177.

least not in the traditional sense. Yet the term *nonfiction* would also be a misnomer, for Cézanne and his work serve only as a backdrop before which Handke's development as an artist in the late 1970s is sketched. Indeed, Handke points out in his interview with June Schlueter that for him writing is merely a "narrative posture" that creates "the impression of fiction. . . . But these narratives and novels really have no story. They are only daily occurrences brought into a new order."[10]

Like *Slow Journey Home, Sainte Victoire* exemplifies Germany's New Sensibility; in this book Handke delves into himself and examines his subjective relationship to art and life. But here, as in the later *Children's Story,* his style assumes the biblical quality hinted at in his previous novel. Handke's prose is replete with antiquated words and phrases, with syntactical constructions straight from the last century. The book is nevertheless both a continuation and exegesis of *Slow Journey Home.* Sorger's conversion from an isolated inwardness to a renewed interest in culture and history as thoroughly human forms is presumed. This book, too, treats Handke's disturbed relationship to the outerworld and to potential new myths that might reinterpret our being in the world. Through Cézanne's art, Handke attempts to break out of the strictures of his individuality and to experience directly the world of objects, bypassing the customary mediation of language and conceptual analysis—just as Cézanne painted through his perceptual notions to capture once more a living sense of the real.

Unlike Sorger's challenge in *Slow Journey Home,* however, Handke's endeavor in *Sainte Victoire* concerns not personal salvation but that of objects as such. Not that these two possibilities are mutually exclusive: for the new synthesis that plagued Sorger has now become a clear goal for Handke, who seeks a mystical unity of self and things, a relinking of the outerworld and the innerworld capable of saving objects from the threat of transience. Cézanne had shown that concentration neither on pure form nor on individual

10. Ibid., 172.

objects would alone be adequate. What is needed is a mystical synthesis of both through art: "What counted was always the particular object. Colors and shapes without objects were too little—the objects in their everyday intimacy, too much. . . . Validity could only be found in normal things which, however, the painter had placed in the realm of the extraordinary—and which I now call the 'magic things' " (p. 18).

Cézanne had attempted to "realize" (Handke uses the French word *réalisation*) mundane objects in their purity and innocence: "The apple, the cliff, the human face; that which was real was the attained form" that represented "being in peace" (p. 21). For Handke, this synthesis of universal and particular, of form and content, results in a state of being in repose, the harmony that is the goal of all true art. Thus, Cézanne has led Handke to the realization that he must be committed "to the realm of form as a different order of things in which 'the true ideas . . . agree with their objects' " (p. 26). In the chaotic realm of the particular, of the unrestrained factual, there can be unity and meaning. This must be posited by an act of artistic creation. Handke describes it as *freiphantasieren*, liberating through imagination.

Handke's study of Cézanne inspires him to retrace the great master's footsteps through southern France, particularly to one mountain of the Sainte Victoire range that had often commanded the painter's fascinated attention and was present in many of his late works. Consequently, the author undertakes a journey on foot from Aix through Le Tholonet in order to study the mountain and one spot in particular, a fissure in the surface that had captivated Cézanne's imagination.

Handke views this spot in a state of dreamlike contemplation and suddenly, as if struck by a great force, imagines himself inside the fissure and the fissure inside himself. The resulting mystical experience, a unity of object and spirit, produces knowledge, understanding, and the ability to express this feeling: "I saw the realm of words open itself to me—with the Great Spirit of Form, the cloak of security: the interval of invulnerability for 'the indeterminate duration of existence,' as the philosopher has defined it" (p. 115). All things surrounding and involved in this experience—the people, landscape, and sky—become familiar to Handke; now he feels "the structure of all these things in me, as my mental equipment" (p. 116) for future writing, for capturing *this* experience. Thus, the poet as seer has in this vision sensed the mystical unity of particular and universal, of object and form, and the experience becomes the foundation for his art.

The book's concluding chapter, a word picture of the woods near Salzburg apparently unrelated to Handke's study of Cézanne, attempts to provide a natural description adequate to his newly found Cézanne-like comprehension of the individual's relationship with nature. The entire thrust of the chapter, including its tone and style, stand in stark contrast to the emotional soul-searching of the rest of the book. But it would be wrong to criticize this chapter, as some have done, as strangely incompatible with what precedes. *The Lesson of Sainte Victoire* is no more a book about Cézanne than it is a book about a French mountain range. Rather, it is the study of the writer's relationship as artist with the knowable world. Is the writer a seer, a creator and grantor of myth with near universal validity? Or is the kind of mystical experience Handke describes relegated to the private sphere, with little bearing on the cognitive facility of other people? Critics have pointed out that Handke has chosen Spinoza, the pantheistic philosopher of the seventeenth century who believed in the oneness of God and nature, as his mentor. Handke's visionary thought and elliptical style betray his preference for an earlier time, for an age when idealistic philosophy reigned supreme. Both *Slow Journey Home* and *The Lesson of Sainte Victoire* work to subvert the perniciously antihumanistic progress of science and scientific thought—geology plays an important role in both books—by proposing a synthesis of twentieth-century positivist thought with the idealism of a past era. Both Sorger (whose name entertains the punnish possibilities of *sich sorgen*, to worry, and *sorgen für*, to take care of) in *Slow Journey* and the nameless narrator in *Sainte Victoire* represent this attempt; both stake out a new being-in-the-world between the realm of pure objects and the self-centered solipsism inherent in the pure inwardness that threatened Sorger at the start.

Handke certainly sees *The Lesson of Sainte Victoire* as a step beyond *Slow Journey Home.* Whereas Sorger-Handke of *Slow Journey* never accomplishes his return home, *Sainte Victoire* begins with the following sentence: "Back in Europe I needed the language of everyday life and read many things anew" (p. 9). But as the book is a history of Handke's fascination with Cézanne, so is it also a portrayal of the genesis of *Slow Journey Home.* That book, which in *Sainte Victoire* is called "the story of the man with the crossed arms" (a reference to a painting by Cézanne), is explicitly mentioned no fewer than fifteen times. Yet in a greater sense, the spirit of *Slow Journey Home* is the driving force behind *The Lesson of Sainte Victoire.* Many writers have found it necessary to explain their work in a subsequent book, but this is not Handke's intention. The difficulty in portraying the immediacy of the experiences that he had lived through led him to choose as his protagonist a scientist, a geologist—at a time when Handke himself was delving seriously into geology—and to place this character in an unreal world, far from everyday concerns. Readers accustomed to seeing the author in Handke's main characters will have trouble finding his familiar literary personality, in its closest applications, here. Yet the genesis of the abrupt break in Handke's work between *The Left-Handed Woman* and *Slow Journey Home* demanded a historical dimension, and *The Lesson of Sainte Victoire* provides just that personal bridge.

Children's Story (1981, as yet untranslated) continues Handke's line of development in the style and mood of the New Sensibility. In this book, the object of contemplation is neither the earth's forms nor works of art but Handke's own child. In this perhaps most autobiographical of Handke's books, the narrator (clearly Handke himself) tells the story of his relationship with his daughter from her birth to about age ten. But the book's purely autobiographical quality is somewhat obscured by the author's refusal to name his characters, himself and his daughter—they are simply called "the man" and "the child" or "the grown-up" and "the growing child." As in *The Lesson of Sainte Victoire,* nevertheless, the degree of fiction is hard to determine, for Handke—in pursuit of myths—tells his story in the most general of terms, using a style at once biblical and romantic while introducing a new conceptual framework. It is a rare author who has the nerve to claim that he is "working on the secret of the world" (p. 91), as Handke does, or to add that "he knew the truth and was pervaded by the obligation to transmit this truth" (p. 23) for "gradually it became a certainty that, for people like him, a different world history has always been valid" (pp. 23–24).

Of course this world history is quite different from that which we find in history books: not a record of facts, but one of myth and its linkage to the human community—a history accessible only to the poet, the prophet, the seer; a history not of change but of constancy, of eternal laws with universal validity. Whereas in Handke's two previous books the forms of the earth and then the shapes and colors of Cézanne's art provided impetus to find and pursue the call of providence, now the child offers him insight into the eternal myth-giving laws of the universe. In one instance, the narrator is able to read the forms of world history "which appeared to him in the lines of the sleeping child" (p. 24). In another, when he is observing his daughter in the garden, the narrator is overwhelmed by the moment's mythical quality: "Such moments should never pass or be forgotten. They demand perpetuality: musical strains, epic song" (p. 136).

Not that the narrator had always been a great lover of children; on the contrary, he had been accustomed to see them as the "cruel-merciless tribe 'that takes no prisoners'—barbaric and cannibalistic" (p. 122). On the other hand, Peter Handke had always been consumed by the need for a child of his own—he felt it was part of his calling. "Just the fact 'child,' without special characteristics, radiated joy—innocence was a form of the spirit" (p. 10). Gradually Handke's relationship with his daughter deepened, and when he and his wife separated Handke took custody of the child. The following years saw the author vacillating between desolation and fulfillment. Instead of pursuing his work, Handke was able to use his daughter as his "excuse before the current problems of world history" (p. 20). His life and work took on the ambience of a world consisting largely of "children's sounds and children's things," of "daily routine running its course in the rhythm of children's time," as life acquired a feeling of "brutal and senseless destiny" (p. 50). Dealing with the all-consuming daily needs of a child had robbed Handke of his special sense for colors and shapes as well as for the "distance and gradation of things" (p. 52). Handke's carefully constructed world of intellect, the world that had been conceived to become a counterweight to the banality of modern times, begins to dissolve, and with it Handke's feeling of proportion, detachment, and decency. In one scene, he lets a minor annoyance bring him into a rage in which he hits his daughter almost hard enough to kill her.

Yet life with a child provides Handke with experiences that offer him insight into the secrets of being. Watching his child walk through a park, he knows that in this mystical moment "a general law has been resolved whose form it was his duty to bring to light and which will only be binding upon others in its appropriate form. And he knows that liberating in thought the sequence of forms inherent in such a moment is the most difficult human undertaking possible" (p. 33).

His daughter provides Handke with the impulses that Sorger found in the forms of the earth and that Handke earlier discovered in Cézanne's art: the unity of self and other, of fulfillment within society and history. Watching a group of children on their way to school, Handke feels a similar impulse; at such times he knows that the modern era he had despised and cursed no longer existed. "Even the *Endzeit* [End of Being] was a chimera: with each new consciousness new and similar possibilities began, and the eyes of the children—look at them!—transmitted the eternal spirit" (p. 126).

In a recent interview, Handke described the process that led him to write *Children's Story,* how he came to view children as symbols for "the law of the world" as he calls it. As if to underline the mythical content of his book, he stresses the formal parallel he constructed between Thucidides' history of the Peloponnesian War and his *Children's Story:* "I thought I would like to tell the story of one person just as one would tell the story of an entire people—what it flowers to, what it can unfold to, what possibilities a person has, as if he were an entire people—and he is an entire people."[11] Handke's interest in classical antiquity stems from his belief that history, especially the history of art, can provide him with the formal possibilities appropriate to his view of art and the world. And classical antiquity has managed to demonstrate the universality he envisions for his own art: "Thus *Children's Story* arose; it is a story of today and of all times" (p. 10). In this manner, the obstacles of language are overcome, and fiction, stripped of its outdated and distracting conventions, can more directly serve human needs, not the least being its author's own.

The redemptive aspect of Handke's work, which was particularly apparent in *Slow Journey Home,* assumes its most compelling form in *Through the Villages* (1981, as yet untranslated), the fourth and final of Handke's homecoming works. *Through the Villages,* as a minimally dramatic play, continues the developmental line that Handke began in *The Weight of the World,* in which for the first time myth and its connections to history, art, nature, and human community were invoked. This is not to suggest that the author has now abandoned his study of language and its cognitive function. On the contrary, this interest still occupies a central position in his thought as well as in his writing: Handke continues to believe in the redemptive force of poetic language—a key theme in *Through the Villages*. We must keep in mind that language is a vital mediating link between the individual and nature (as outerworld) as well as between

11. Krista Fleischmann, "Ein Gespäch über das Schrieben und die Kindergeschichte," *Die Rampe* 2 (1981): 9.

the individual and his fellow man. For cognition of the outerworld, expression of this "other" is possible only through the appropriation of its structures in their form as language. In *The Weight of the World* Handke notes, "When in the course of the day language arises, becomes, comes to consciousness, is found: Revitalization of dead nature" (p. 310), and thereby emphasizes this critical function of the poetic. Only the poet, in possession of his own language infused with his subjectivity, can reach his fellow man and effect a change. As Handke told June Schlueter, "There is a sigh of relief through the masses when there is someone who has language." Language, Handke argues, is form, and "form is permanence, because otherwise there is no permanence in human existence."[12] This desire to affect his fellow man "contagiously" is perhaps the reason Handke chose the stage, a more public form of expression, for *Through the Villages,* a play that addresses the problems of alienated existence devoid of meaning, lacking any access to universality in nature and history.

Handke first conceived his play as a three-hour monologue. Later, he opted for a more conventional format, finally publishing *Through the Villages* as a dramatic poem (the play's subtitle) in four scenes performed by ten actors. Unlike his early plays, which in discarding traditional modes of theatrical representation and attempting to subvert the theater as an institution faithfully representing social reality create a world totally concrete and self-apparent, *Through the Villages* invokes the theater's historical tradition. It returns to the Greek stage in search of inspirational models that might provide a vehicle to portray universality of form and myth. "I don't think that great art or universality is at all possible any longer today," he argued in the *Die Rampe* interview, "if one doesn't go all the way back and study form through all the centuries."[13]

In *Through the Villages* Handke resumes the homecoming motif he had introduced in *Slow Journey Home.* The brother

12. Schlueter, *Plays and Novels of Peter Handke,* p. 173.

13. Fleischmann, "Ein Gespäch über des Schrieben und die Kindergeschicte," 9.

and sister who had concerned Sorger in that novel now enter the play as full characters. But the striking banality of plot is underscored and counterpointed by the exalted language of the dramatis personae, largely villagers and construction workers, who speak in tones unheard since the demise of classical drama. "Great spirit of the cosmos, descend this day upon us" says Hans, one of the workers and the hero's brother, "reveal yourself in the broad and airy realm; let us hover above the earth and lift, as the top of a parachute, the innermost of our breasts" (p. 33).

Gregor, the play's central figure, returns to his natal village (the final leg of the journey home) after a long absence abroad (just as Handke returned to Austria after a decade's residence in West Germany and France). His return is prompted by his brother's request that Gregor, the eldest of the three children and heir to their recently deceased parents' property in the village, agree to mortgage the house and land so that their sister, Sophie, a clerk in a local store, can start her own business. At first Gregor resists, horrified at the rampant industrialization that has swept over village and countryside since his departure. He has until this point felt little love for his siblings; now he sees his parents' property, their life's work, as a spiritual anchor in a world threatened by transition and fragmentation. Even the village, once isolated and therefore sheltered from commercialization, has become the target of developers: "I see on every worker's house in every village, no matter how isolated it is, company and bank signs glittering and for business houses nowhere a countryside. I see no empty paths and no access to the free plain. I see my lack of responsibility and my betrayal. . . . I can only preserve. And that is what I intend to do: preserve at any price" (pp. 18–19). The village, once a haven in which man and nature lived in peace, has been disturbed by "the evil discord of business." Gregor responds with "a dream: I saw this property, freed from danger, with the blue sky above it, and thought: 'I have saved a piece of land. I have saved a piece of heaven' " (p. 61).

But Gregor's plan is, at least in part, nullified by the

construction work of his brother, Hans, who travels from valley to valley, building gigantic projects of steel and concrete, defiling the primeval nature of the countryside. In the lives of these country people, torn loose from the traditional rural signification system of myth, tradition, and nature, Gregor sees reflected on a small scale the problems that plague western civilization—and that have inspired Handke's work: alienation, roothlessness, meaninglessness. As if to underscore this condition, the workers chant a hymn to despair, for which the stage directions prescribe a sing-song tone:

> When will the man with the scripture return to me my rights?
> When will I be able to wish instead of desiring victory?
> . . . .
> When will the singer with his cheerful voice stop the flood of rainfall
> and banish into antiquity the raging blood of guilt and damnation in people's breasts?
> When will the episodically tinkling bells boom as eternity and humanity live on the earth?
>
> (pp. 49–50)

This chant of the workers gradually degenerates into an orgy of hate and despair.

Gregor takes the cry for a poet-redeemer to heart. He comprehends his desire to save his parents' property as futile in the face of so much need. He gives in to his sister and brother and allows Sophie to carry out her plan. Yet Gregor's decision is motivated not by a sense of reconciliation but by despair: "We are only we as losers," he concluded. "We are the descendants of losers who, like great wheels of cheese, rolled into their graves, and we, in a similar fashion, will roll after them, each by himself" (p. 85). He turns to Hans's little son and says, "He will be a slave like his father and his grandfather, and he will produce the next slave without a second thought, who will in turn bring coming generations into the world" (p. 86). Gregor concludes, "You relatives, you are the evil ones" (p. 87). The world collapses in his speech as well as in the workers' speeches. Hans agrees with his brother: "There is neither knowledge nor certainty. There is nothing whole, and what I think, I think alone, and what occurs to me alone is not truth, but opinion" (p. 93).

Gregor, who upon arriving in the village had perceived a glimpse of hope, thus finds only despair. And his despair is transferred to the workers and village people. The play threatens to end in an orgy of hate and despondency, but Handke introduces a device, a kind of deus ex machina, that turns things around to conclude with an air of hope. Nova ("the spirit of the new age," as she is called throughout), Gregor's mysterious, Cassandra-like companion on his journey home, climbs the steps of a ladder placed against the wall of the village cemetery, where the last scene is set. She launches into a moral panegyric, strongly reminiscent of the Sermon on the Mount, addressed to the collected villagers and workers. Nova, who had described Gregor as a man "with an ear for the subterranean choir of longing for home," "a wanderer without a shadow" (p. 91) and who had counseled him to be the example that could lead the villagers to meaning ("Show your eyes, beckon others to the profound. . . . Go through the villages. I will follow you," pp. 19–20), now offers hope and invokes in nature openness and range as exemplary guidance. She advises that being and nonbeing should not be brooded about, for "being *is*" (p. 96); that gratitude is a permanence from which, as love, one can affect fellowman; that beauty and illusion, created by humans, are the deeply moving components of being that can change people and cause them to rethink their existence: "Illusion is the power of vision, and vision is true" (p. 101). At this point her audience removes the masks they had donned prior to her monologue—a gesture symbolic of openness and incipient transformation.

"Cease your brooding," Nova preaches, "whether God or not God: the one makes us dizzy unto death, and other kills imagination, and without imagination no matter becomes form: this is the God who is valid for all. Becoming aware and moulding form heals matter" (p. 103). Nova concludes with an apodictic affirmation of existence infused with hope, made possible by beauty, art, and form: "The form is the law, and the law is great, and it elevates you. The heaven is great. The village is great. Eternal peace is possible. . . . Hold firm to this dramatic poem. Go eternally toward your goal. Go through the villages" (p. 106). The play concludes with Nova descending from her elevated position above the cemetery (perhaps implying transcendence over death as well as a connectedness via tradition and history with past generations) and placing a crown on the head of Hans's son, suggesting that the son will become the new man whose very existence, transcending the tribulations of everyday life, will, as "the child of peace" (p. 102) invoked by Nova, successfully struggle and achieve a new comprehension of peace, beauty, nature, and art that can serve as an impetus to transformation for others.

Handke, who in 1971 abandoned the stage as a literary arena, in 1981 returned to the theater not as a brash, young innovator but as a mature writer with a message of human redemption through art and nature. As such a message, *Through the Villages* is the culmination of the process—Handke's search for myth and form—initiated in *The Weight of the World* and intensively realized in *Slow Journey Home, The Lesson of Sainte Victoire,* and *Children's Story.* Whereas Handke's earlier drama reveled in its hermetic self-apparency, its sense of play, and its insistent refusal to bear a message, *Through the Villages* represents the attempt to give public expression to his new understanding of the human condition, to effect change in his audience.

V. Drama and Poetry as the Limits of Revolt

> You are now aware of your presence. You know that it is *your* time that you are spending here. You are the topic. You tie the knot. You untie the knot. You are the center. You are the occasion. You are the reason why.
>
> —*Offending the Audience*

Peter Handke's progress with the novel has been exceptional, spanning the full range of postmodern revolt, redirection, and adjustment of mainstream concerns. It would be remarkable indeed to see him maintain his early promise as an inspired writer in the three major genres, forging new identities for drama and poetry as well as fiction. That midway through his career he shifted nearly all his attention to novels, however, does not mean that his once-notorious poems and plays were a misdirection. Instead, they remain important on several counts: as an index to the great amount of literary reinvention awaiting bright young writers in the early 1960s; as exercises in even clearer form for the linguistic and artistic theory Handke was applying to fiction during these years; and, most instructively, as an indication of how poetry and drama were more quickly depleted in Handke's quest to "ship myself and my headaches off to market as a commodity" (*A Sorrow Beyond Dreams*, p. 30).

The most obvious fact is that his poems and plays have been more starkly elemental, lacking the quotidian base that, after first seeming so impossible, has come to dominate each succeeding novel. From *The Hornets* through *Children's Story*, Handke has turned inward to include both more of his own life and more of his most private feelings, all the while maintaining the rigid axioms of a postmodern aesthetic that allow no compromise with the now untruthful conventions of traditional art. Drama and poetry, within the tradition, would seem to offer even more scope for inwardness. But for Handke they haven't; instead, their conventions were obstacles to overturn as he worked out his own practice of the postmodern aesthetic. It is interesting to note the programmatic nature of this progression, especially in Handke's drama; after a careful step-by-step exhaustion of theatrical conventions, he turned to a decade of maturely complex fiction, only returning to drama with *Über die Dörfer* to make his explorations of the New Sensibility complete.

At the beginning of our study, we cited Handke's fascination with the comparative nature of man's perceptual processes: objects seem to exist only so that they can be played off against each other and thereby create "meaning," which is of course something quite apart from what actually exists in the world. Through the process of comparing, we not only refuse to perceive the thing as it is; we also create a hierarchy of objects in our consciousness in which each new perception finds its niche. Hence, we form what Michel Foucault calls systems of constraint, the constituting of so-called objective systems of knowledge, which in fact institute subjection to a particular historical or political frame of meaning.[1]

This situation is paradigmatic for Handke's attack on conventional theater. By its physical nature, drama is even more naturally mimetic than fiction, summoning forth our most common habits of perception. As Handke sees it, the theatergoer watches a set of actions and listens to a set of dialogues, both of which can be readily compared with situations and conversations known from outside the theater. In traditional drama, reality as staged represents a reality that exists outside the theater building, and the viewers are encouraged to compare theatrical experience with their preformed notions about the real world. Handke's use of the stage is a radical attempt to disrupt this traditional relationship. This subversion of form is especially apparent in the early *Sprechstücke*, or speak-ins, but applies as well to

1. Karlis Racevskis, *Michel Foucault and the Subversion of Intellect* (Ithaca: Cornell University Press, 1983), pp. 15–16.

the later, more superficially traditional plays. In *Offending the Audience* (1966), for example, the audience is ushered into the theater with great solemnity, as if being graciously invited to their customary theater experience of well-dressed and thoughtfully attentive formality. Then the curtain opens to reveal a group of "speakers," standing about on an empty stage, who immediately destroy the viewers' illusions about any play they might have expected. The speakers explain that they are there to observe the audience and its reactions—that the audience will provide the play's theme and action, in a reversal of the dramatic tradition.

This style of role reversal is central to many of Handke's plays. What begins as a simple mechanism, however, soon proves itself as an important reinvention of drama. Recalling the success of *Offending the Audience* with audiences at large, Handke described how such direct address is actually more real than conventional forms of representation:

> All you have to do is turn to the spectators and start off; with a perfectly simple shift of ninety degrees you have a new play, a new dramaturgy. Everybody wanted to see it—out of curiosity, perhaps out of a certain masochism. The secret was that people still expected something of the theatre. The kind of immediacy film can't achieve. Now they suddenly felt that theatre spoke directly to them and that this was what they had been missing. Most normal plays disappoint the spectator because they really have nothing to do with his situation in the outside world: they only refer to specific individuals. The dramaturgy doesn't speak to the spectators. The course of events, the mechanics of the dialogue aren't attuned to their acute problems. The dramaturgy is a hundred years old; it runs behind the reality of the day like a rusty bicycle, a tandem. Theatregoers feel that. To put it in geometrical terms: this rectangular relationship, in which people onstage talk to each other while others watch them, is outdated.[2]

Handke therefore considers it essential to the life of drama that the illusionary character of the modern play be replaced

2. Artur Joseph, "Nauseated by Language: From an Interview with Peter Handke," *The Drama Review* 15 (Fall 1970): 58–59.

with something more self-apparently real. His plays make clear that the events onstage represent nothing outside the theater—they merely represent themselves. Language and experience are the content of Handke's drama, which attempts to reconquer a corrupted reality through language, all by means of a systematic critique of language as the vehicle of perception (and therefore of reality's making).

Early plays such as *Offending the Audience, Calling for Help, Prophecy, Self-Accusation,* and *Kaspar* (dating from 1966 and 1967) fit this mode of linguistic deconstruction. With *My Foot My Tutor* (1969), Handke reaches a turning point, at which he feels able to abandon language altogether. From here on, Handke's stage assigns itself the task of examining situations rather than language per se. *The Ride Across Lake Constance* (1971) and *They Are Dying Out* (1973) embody the logical consequence of his earlier experimentation. These plays create in the viewer an eerie sense of uncertainty, of radical unfamiliarity. The audience sees actors acting, but the actions onstage do not correspond to anything in the viewers' repertory of personal experience. Instead, these plays create a full reality of their own, complexly constructive rather than mechanically deconstructive. Again, there is no reference to anything outside the theater, but a fully formed yet nonillusionistic world is being made on stage. It is possible that Handke's theater represents a turn to radical realism, for the playwright has thought out realism to its logical extreme: his plays create something that is totally and concretely real *in itself.* The viewer has no choice but to accept the scene as presented—without comparing, without introducing the experience into an already present cognitive hierarchy. Thus, Handke's plays develop in the theatergoer a tension arising from the contradiction between what is being seen and what is known from experience. This tension, moreover, creates a heightened sense of awareness, not only drawing attention to the dramatic processes but calling into question traditional modes of expression and understanding. These plays thus attempt to destroy our traditional role consciousness, within which we experience the world as individuals yet with a preconceived notion of reality. Above all, Handke sees his style of theater as natural rather than contrived:

> I haven't tried to create forms. Because of the need to express a particular content certain forms necessarily emerged. I never intended to be an innovator, and if I did it was a superficial attitude. . . . In *The Ride Across Lake Constance* I believe that there is a consciousness going beyond theatre, a precisely formulated consciousness of communication and of difficulties—difficulties with living. The other plays were purely theatrical, without any real reference point. They made it too easy for lazy consciousnesses to "see the enemy."[3]

Midway through Peter Handke's first play, *Offending the Audience,* his actors explain to the audience just what it has been witnessing:

> This piece is a prologue. It is not the prologue to another piece but the prologue to what you did, what you are doing, and what you will do. You are the topic. This piece is the prologue to the topic. It is the prologue to your practices and customs. It is the prologue to your actions. It is the prologue to your inactivity. It is the prologue to your lying down, to your sitting, to your standing, to your walking. It is the prologue to the plays and to the seriousness of your life. It is also the prologue to your future visits to the theatre. It is also the prologue to all other prologues. This piece is world theatre. (p. 28)

Block paragraphs such as this fill forty pages of the play's printed text and reflect what action the play allows: a line of actors standing at the stage's edge, addressing the audience with declarative statements about the theatrical experience they are sharing. Throughout, there have been disclaimers about the play's antirepresentational nature, about how the words of this drama "don't point at the world as something lying outside the words but to the world in the words themselves" (p. ix). This one basic notion is repeated in virtually every line of the play, becoming in fact its action: to

3. Jack Zipes, "Contrary Positions: An Interview with Peter Handke," *Performance* 1 (September–October 1972): 63.

reeducate the audience to a new set of theatrical conventions, based upon language rather than on mime, and on the reality of significations in themselves instead of as indicators of something else. Handke's *Sprechstücke* "have no action, since every action on the stage would only be the picture of another action." Virtually every dramatic convention is overturned by this new arrangement; traditional theater will never be the same. "Speak-ins are autonomous prologues to the old plays," Handke explains. "They do not want to revolutionize, but to make aware" (p. ix).

So line after line of *Offending the Audience* works to remind the audience of just those things it would prefer to forget. Dramatic actions, which are used to represent something else, have always been things in themselves—now they are deliberately used that way, as if for the very first time. Words in language are signifiers, a coded representation of another object in the real world, yet they do have their own material existence—Handke's writing dramatizes this fact, in a self-consciously instructional manner. Both cast and audience are conditioned to this new awareness. The actors are told to listen to Catholic litanies, football cheers, rock lyrics, song titles on the hit parade: all examples of words being themselves rather than transparent windows to another reality. As the audience enters the theater, it is "greeted by the usual pre-performance atmosphere"—backstage noises, scenery shifts, whispers by stagehands and managers, movements of the ushers—all amplified and stylized so as to draw attention to the theatrical experience; in Handke's play, however, these functions are not real but are instead "make-believe" (p. 4). This inversion prepares the audience for its complement in the spoken part of the play, in which there will be no make-believe, only words spoken by the actors to the people in the house.

The first words are just that, words, written and spoken in a way that emphasizes acoustic pattern over meaning, with no other picture being produced:

> You will hear nothing you have not heard here before.
> You will see nothing you have not seen here before.

You will see nothing of what you have always seen here.
You will hear nothing of what you have always heard here.
(p. 7)

Notice that while the semantic meaning of these sentences is virtually identical, the words and their arrangement are different. By using such repetitions, Handke is schooling theatergoers in the materiality of language, showing them where to direct their attention. Anyone intent upon discovering meaning through action will soon be frustrated; only by responding to the words as things in themselves might there be variety, interest, and dramatic action.

So, too, for the set. "These boards don't signify a world," the actors say. "They are part of the world. These boards exist for us to stand on. This world is no different from yours" (p. 9). "This stage represents nothing," they continue in the next block paragraph. "It represents no other emptiness. This stage *is* empty" (p. 10). What is the event of this drama? The audience itself—which is soon reminded of how it dressed for the theater, traveled across town, waited in line, entered the theater, was seated, and sat in expectation just moments before the play began. "The time here is *your* time," the audience is told. "Space time here is your space time. . . . The umbilical cord connecting you to your time is not severed here" (p. 15). There are still representations, but for this play they are located among the audience, which has costumed itself for an occasion, made allowances in its normal order for this special event of coming to the theater, has been seated in a carefully arranged plan, and in general has allowed itself to be transformed by the unities of time, place, and action. "Therefore this piece is classical," the actors whimsically claim (p. 20).

Having realized it is the play's subject, the audience is next run through an actor's regimen: "Try not to blink your eyelids. Try not to swallow any more. Try not to move your tongue. Try not to hear anything" (p. 21). Does this make the experience of drama different? Quite so, Handke insists, recalling that under the old rules the theatrical experience had nearly suffocated beneath its outmoded, lifeless conventions. "You looked at dead points. You experienced a dead time. You heard a dead language" (p. 23). All of these actions are now made to live again, just as in Handke's novels the simplest acts of realistic behavior are transformed into life-or-death adventures as his characters struggle to find themselves within a suddenly desystematized existence. Traditional drama, it may be argued, never really existed as itself: "The play was not played for the play's sake but for the sake of reality" (p. 24), and under those circumstances who would prefer a counterfeit to the real thing? Handke's new style of theater has the chance to be richer than reality, for in his drama, the audience is told, "The impossibilities of your dreams do not have to confine themselves to the possibilities of the stage. . . . The absurdity of your dreams does not have to obey the authentic laws of the theatre" (p. 27). Hence, drama is reinvented, restructured in a way that should make it much more potent than it was in its illusionistic, representational form.

Peter Handke's aversion for representation and his preference for the representational system as a fully independent thing in itself marks him as a postmodernist, in an age away from the philosophically similar but technically conventional dramas of the early Samuel Beckett, Harold Pinter, and Edward Albee. His superficially Beckettian *Self-Accusation* takes a situation familiar from plays and novels of the 1940s and 1950s and reshapes it by an attention to language. Again, an acoustic order is what Handke has in mind; though realistically just one person's monologue, in *Self-Accusation* it is spoken by two actors—one male, the other female—with abrupt transitions meant to destroy the illusion of an integral character and instead reinforce the universal language of their statements. "I came into the world," reads the first of several dozen paragraphs, which increase in length and in complexity (both in structure and in subject) as they grow in years of experience. In each, an initial line is run through variations that are largely linguistic:

> I looked. I saw objects. I looked at indicated objects. I indicated indicated objects. I learned the designation of indicated objects. I designated indicated objects. I learned the

designation of objects which cannot be indicated. I learned. I remembered. I remembered the signs I learned. I saw designated forms. I designated similar forms with the same name. I designated differences between dissimilar forms. I designated absent forms. I learned to fear absent forms. I learned to wish for the presence of absent forms. I learned the words "to wish" and "to fear." (p. 37)

As each speaker grows, he or she is initiated into "mankind's historic rules" (p. 39); soon the succeeding block paragraphs consist of rules that have been violated and expressions of disregard, as affairs become quite complicated, especially linguistically:

> I expressed approval in places where the expression of approval was prohibited. I expressed disapproval at times when the expression of disapproval was not desired. I expressed disapproval and approval in places and at times when the expression of disapproval and the expression of approval were intolerable. I failed to express approval at times when the expression of approval was called for. I expressed approval during a difficult trapeze act in the circus. I expressed approval inopportunely. (p. 42)

Names are assigned to certain concepts, adding one layer of abstraction on another as personality is formed ("I called conclusions futuristic. I called integrity intellectual. I called capitalism corrupt," p. 45). Actions accrue, others lapse, as a human being creates a presence in the world ("I did not eradicate evil at its roots. I irresponsibly thrust children into the world," p. 49). For all its promise, for all its cumulative effects, life is a thing of diminishment: "I am not what I was. I was not what I should have been. I did not become what I should have become. I did not keep what I should have kept" (p. 51). Above all, the experience is not a representation. It has been real, as the piece concludes: "I went to the theatre. I heard this piece. I spoke this piece. I wrote this piece" (p. 51).

If *Self-Accusation* dramatizes the natural linguistic evolution of a life, Handke's first evening-filling *(abendfüllen)* work, *Kaspar* (1967, translated 1969) examines the same situation with a beginning in medias res. The protagonist "owns one sentence," which is: "I want to be a person like somebody else once was" (p. 72). Kaspar, a young man from the country, has arrived in town with this single statement; everything else in the play, and in his life, grows from it, just as the words of *Self-Accusation* all followed from its initial sentence of birth. The subject of *Kaspar* is more properly linguistic, for growth will be measured in language and language only. A prologue titled "Kaspar's Sixteen Phases" shows the ideality of this development: beginning with one sentence, Kaspar must first use it alone, then use it against other sentences (and so become aware of what he speaks), "bring himself into order with sentences about order," find a model sentence and so develop a generative grammar, and—most crucially—project with "rhyme and reason" a similar rhyme and reason onto the things he sees.

Breaking through the rear curtain to the stage, Kaspar is the picture of astonishment. He repeats his sentence by rote, not knowing what its parts mean or how they function together; although the sentence sounds all right, Kaspar's inability to use it is indicated by his similarly awkward attempts to walk (the parts of his body refuse to work in harmony). As he stumbles about the stage full of props, the play's prompters begin to tell him what to do. "Already you have a sentence with which you can make yourself noticeable," they begin. "The sentence is more useful to you than a word," they counsel, because the sentence can be spoken with style to express meaning (p. 67). "You have a sentence you can place between yourself and everything else," and by doing this Kaspar "will exercise every disorder" (p. 69). What he says, he thinks; order is thus created. When Kaspar resists the prompters' instructions, his deliberate garbling of his sentence soon results in a new one—he has used language to place himself against their world and hence create a new one of his own. But this soon proves a trap, for the prompters seize his initiative and use it to teach him names for things, their functions, and even clichés about their use and behavior (a parody of superstitions and prejudices passed from generation to generation). Kaspar soon learns the mixed blessings of language:

> Ever since I can speak I can stand up in a normal fashion; but falling only hurts ever since I can speak; but the pain when I fall is half as bad as ever since I know that I can speak about the pain; but falling is twice as bad as ever since I know that one can speak about my falling; but falling doesn't hurt at all any more ever since I know that I can forget the pain; but the pain doesn't stop at all any more ever since I know that I can feel ashamed of falling. (p. 79)

"The first order has been created" (p. 80), Handke's stage directions indicate. That order is a system activated by language; and, as Kaspar notes, the speaker can control language only to the extent of initiating it—after which it systematically takes care of itself, with all the logical consequences for the speaker. Kaspar orders the stage, so that everything goes with everything else. He is prompted on the arbitrary workings of metaphor and concept: "The door has two sides: truth has two sides: if the door had three sides, truth would have three sides" (p. 90). The logic of the system rules all, even to the extent of speaking. "When you begin to speak you will begin to think what you speak," the prompters advise, "even when you want to think something different" (p. 100). Kaspar tries to list the rules, but several other Kaspars soon fill the stage to frustrate his designs and mock his efforts—for there is, after all, a chaos to existence that language cannot fully control. Problems of the one and the many are unsolvable. This chaotic life goes on, while Kaspar now remains the puppet of his language. "Already with my first sentence," he admits, "I was trapped" (p. 137).

In choosing Kaspar as his main character, Handke has placed himself in a long German tradition of fascination with the historical figure Kaspar Hauser, who as an autistic child of sixteen appeared under mysterious circumstances in Nuremberg in 1828. At the time of his discovery, Kaspar Hauser supposedly possessed a single sentence, "I would like to become a rider like my father once was." The young man, who had been raised in a closet apart from nearly all human contact, quickly became a romantic cause célèbre, and his story has been treated by writers as diverse as Karl

Gutzkow, Paul Verlaine, Georg Trakl, and Ernst Jandl, whose poem "Sixteen Years" Handke chose as the epigraph to his play. Nor has Handke's work been the last on this subject; in 1975, Werner Herzog made a film, *Every Man for Himself and God against All*, on the Kaspar theme. The name itself is a pun on the word *kasper*, German for *clown*, particularly in the Austrian tradition, in which the clown-figure Kasperl is known to every child.

Yet Handke is just as careful to distance himself from the Kaspar Hauser legend. "The play *Kaspar* does not show how IT REALLY IS or REALLY WAS with Kaspar Hauser," he states at the beginning. "It shows what IS POSSIBLE with someone. It shows how someone can be made to speak through speaking" (p. 59). With their sentences, the prompters teach Kaspar the rules of social propriety—all of which are quite arbitrary, for once his sentences are destroyed, his words make no sense. Kaspar is submitted to "speech torture," as Handke terms it (p. 59) by these disembodied voices that are representatives less of reality per se than they are of social forces, Foucault's systems of constraint. Hence, the prompters have imbued Kaspar with a set of sentences adequate to cope with the world only in a limited and superficial way. Kaspar had learned to conceptualize the world as metaphor; and metaphor, as we have seen in Chapter I, is an artificial transformation of the world, positing a claim that one thing is something else, radically different from what it really is but perceptually instructive in its point of contrast—the reality is less what a thing is than what it isn't. Consequently, language can destroy innocence, distort perception, and serve as an instrument that shapes meaning.

Kaspar was the play that made Handke a major playwright among European audiences. It won its young author the coveted Gerhart Hauptmann Prize, and became the most frequently produced play of the year (quite a contrast to the previous year's most produced author, Shakespeare). *Kaspar* had first been performed at the Theater am Turm in Frankfurt, directed by Clays Peymann; The Other Company in London staged it in 1970. It was *The Ride Across Lake*

Constance, however, that brought Handke his greatest notoriety as a dramatist. It debuted in Berlin on 23 January 1971; one year later, Joseph Papp introduced it to American audiences at New York's Lincoln Center, a reception characterized by boos and hisses. Michael Roloff's translation was published in 1976 with five other pieces: *Prophecy* (1966), *Calling for Help* (1967), *My Foot My Tutor* (1969), *Quodlibet* (1970, and *They Are Dying Out* (1973). A widely reviewed and (in paperback) strong-selling volume, it brought all of Handke's remaining dramatic works into print, making them easily available for study and performance. As a group, they reinforce Handke's argument that traditional forms of literature did not measure truth according to the correspondence of words to the objects described, but instead on whether the objects "correspond to reality," inviting the reader to mistake the words for the objects themselves, something postmodern linguistic theory tells us simply is not so. Moreover, drama had been burdened with unnecessary narrative. For Handke, it has always seemed that the progress of literature consists in the gradual removal of unnecessary fictions. What matters is the communication of experiences, both linguistic and nonlinguistic. Story can be one vehicle for such communication, but not the only one, and it is certainly not necessary to be present in every work at all times.

Prophecy is one of the shorter speak-ins, consisting of anticomparisons listed in series:

> The flies will die like flies.
> The ruttish dogs will snuffle like ruttish dogs.
> The pig on the spit will scream like a pig on the spit.
> The bull will roar as a bull.
>
> (p. 3)

The play at once mocks the human inclination to find truth in comparisons and demonstrates that things are essentially what they are, not something else.

> The stepchild will be treated as a stepchild.
> The miracle worker will be awaited like a miracle worker.
> The freak will be stared at like a freak.
>
> (p. 5)

These are the behavioral consequences of the rules worked out in *Self-Accusation* and made into an educational model in *Kaspar*. Human projections, which the ending of *Kaspar* proved unreliable, are removed in the manner of Alain Robbe-Grillet's phenomenological cleansing. Only the things remain, with these consequences: "Every day will be like every other" (p. 17). There is even a lesson in theater, for a play will no longer be like reality; it will be like a play.

An even more particularized demonstration is found in *Calling for Help*, in which the actors are doing just that—a simple act, which Handke's linguistic perspective and dramatic didacticism make into a mind twister: "While the speakers are seeking the *word* help they are in need of *help;* once having found the word *help* they no longer need any help; before they find the word they ask *for* help, whereas once they have found the word help they only speak *help* without needing to ask *for* help any longer" (p. 21). As always, Handke instructs his actors to use words as they would use them in a soccer chant, for acoustic effect rather than for meaning. Aid is not summoned; rather, the speakers create "an ovation to the word *help*" (p. 22), and in so doing teach the audience a most compelling lesson in language.

My Foot My Tutor is a masterpiece of subtraction: no words, no story, no plot, just actions representing themselves, or drama as pure drama: "the cat," one of the initial props, is free to wander on or off the stage, for "it represents what it does." Like later performance pieces by The Living Theatre and similar groups, Handke's drama is as much concerned with its audience as with a text for the stage; what transpires between the two is more important than either alone (indeed, the two must exist together for drama to happen, an oft-repeated sentiment from *Offending the Audience*). Speech, which has the possibility of transforming reality, often lapses into banality. So do actions, which is exactly what *My Foot My Tutor* demonstrates through a long series of pantomimes between a warden and his ward. Banality results from people wishing too anxiously to interpret, to place meanings upon these actions—whether behavioral or dramatic. Therefore, the play is an exercise in the demystification of acts. An action takes place but is not allowed to signify; instead, it "is repeated so often that it loses its psychological significance" (p. 36). If a character walks across the stage, it is merely to "represent walking" (p. 40). A comic act is performed so slowly that it no longer seems funny; if an actor throws something, he does so "without expressing anything with the manner in which he throws it" (p. 45). The actions are thus made to be simply themselves, which Handke sees as a prerequisite to any future drama.

What *My Foot My Tutor* does with actions, *Quodlibet* does for words. Handke has said that with this latter play he wished to show how people react to single words and sentences and how the resultant aesthetics of perception is expressed in reaction to theatrical forms (p. 58). The meaning of *Quodlibet* is created out of misunderstandings: *napalm* is heard for "no palms," *hero sandwich* instead of "Hiroshima," *cunnilingus* instead of "cunning fingers" (pp. 58–59). Audiences tend to listen to ambiguous words instead of to sentences, Handke points out. Wittgenstein's language theory taught the same principle, that because of verbal confusion we are victimized by our consequently wrongheaded responses; every philosophical problem, he believed, can be traced to language, and Handke agrees. That we live our lives in such constant danger of falling through the thin ice of communication is the premise for *The Ride Across Lake Constance*. The title phrase is a German folk expression, referring to someone who has been in great danger without knowing it—when told, the person dies of shock, even though the danger itself of crossing the lake's thin ice has been survived. Humans trapped within the imperfect system of language are in the same danger every time they speak or are spoken to, since much of functional reality exists within language, not outside of it.

The eight characters of *The Ride Across Lake Constance* converse within a drawing room setting, a set whose deliberate theatricality is enhanced by the characters' names, which in the text are taken from stars of the German stage and screen but which in performance are indicated to be the actors' own. There is no way, therefore, that the viewers' traditional expectations can be fulfilled, for the actors are most apparently actors and not roles to be otherwise represented. Their conversation is random and seemingly pointless; what progress there is happens by misdirection, misunderstanding, and general confusion—all because the speakers are more attuned to the nuances of language than to the simple meanings of words themselves. "Are you dreaming or are you speaking?" asks the play's opening line, and Handke's characters seem to have confused the two. "I caught myself shaking the tablecloth," one character says, and another immediately queries, "Why 'caught'? Why not: 'I saw myself,' 'I noticed'?" (pp. 106–7). Nuances are important, Emil Jannings explains, for once a subject order has been formulated, "People had to stick to it because, after all, they had formulated it" (p. 122). He recalls "a thought of a conversation I had with someone, and I remembered distinctly how he'd smiled when he answered me, and then it occurred to me that I had been talking to him on the telephone!" What does this indicate? That "the manner in which one thinks is determined by the laws of nature" (p. 123). Can anything be unambiguous? Only the language of things themselves, as when one waves money around: "This language he understands!" (p. 126). Pure clarity actually takes the drama out of conversation. "With every one of your feelings you describe to me," one character complains, "you take a possible feeling away from me" (p. 137).

The process of Handke's play is a parody of expected dramatic action: the pacing increases and the action swells toward a climax that never happens (the characters in fact "make themselves small" [p. 159] as if they are freezing), a reminder to the audience that it has been projecting its own expectations onto the stage. We forever struggle to find meanings, even where there are none—both characters and audience have been doing this throughout the play:

> JANNINGS: Someone with an object in his hand begins to squint. Because he has stolen it?

VON STROHEIM: Unless he proves his innocence.

JANNINGS: Someone suddenly puckers up his mouth and nose. *(He shows how.)* Because he's afraid and a coward?

VON STROHEIM: Unless his actions prove the opposite. (p. 177)

The truth of the manner must be constantly reaffirmed:

PORTEN: Someone keeps looking over his shoulder while he's walking. Does he have a guilty conscience?

BERGNER: No, he simply looks over his shoulder from time to time.

PORTEN: Someone is sitting there with lowered head. Is he sad?

BERGNER: *(Assumes a modeling pose for her reply.)* No, he simply sits there with lowered head. (p. 107)

Porten's suppositions are those that students are trained to apply to drama; in turn, those dramatic rules are practiced in life, until people are fully abstracted from the actuality of their behavior—everything must have a *deeper meaning*. Words and gestures are studied for their intent; no one assumes for a moment that intent may be lacking or that words and gestures may simply be representing themselves. Such is the curse of mimesis, which Handke's reinvention of drama hopes to remove.

If we were to believe both his public and literary pronouncements, *They Are Dying Out* would have been Handke's last dramatic piece for some time. The year he was writing this play, 1972, saw the publication of his *Short Letter, Long Farewell*, in which its strongly autobiographical narrator confesses, "It's hard for me . . . to write roles. When I characterize somebody, it seems to me that I'm degrading him. Everything that's individual about him becomes a tic. . . . When I make somebody talk on the stage, he clams up on me after the first few sentences: I've reduced him to a concept. I think maybe I'd do better to write stories" (p. 128). The seemingly pointless business dealings that constitute the dialogue of *They Are Dying Out* fit this description; characters "clam up" before much can be established, and the play lacks even the actor-audience interaction that distinguished Handke's earlier drama. Of all of Handke's work, in any genre, this piece has the most deliberate message: in an anticapitalist diatribe Handke claims that the theory of consumerism camouflages the self and alienates it from others. Reality is defined by one's fictions, Handke has argued from the start, and here that dictum serves to indict the capitalist businessman who defines himself simply by his profit-taking abilities.

The similar conflict of inner lyricism versus outer materialism (and a dead materialism at that) characterizes Peter Handke's poetry. *The Innerworld of the Outerworld of the Innerworld* (1969, translated 1974) is a title that epitomizes Handke's interpretation of the poetic act: as persons act in the world, they engage in a dialectic between their inner feelings and the outward reality within which they exist. There is, of course, much dissembling between the two—the dramatic pieces from the *Lake Constance* collection reaffirm that at every turn. Therefore, the poet must work upon his reader—asking questions, giving instructions, conducting exercises—all to defamiliarize one from the habitual practices obscuring the inner realities of life. "Suggestions for Running Amok" begins with these commands:

> First run through a cornifield.
> Then run through rows in an empty concert hall.
>
> Then, at the end of the football game, try to get back in the stadium through the same entrance.

All three acts are running, and each of the three is a meaningless or objectless running; but Handke's exercise has taught how the three examples are, within their categorical similarity, quite different. Art must recondition, so that the true processes of behavior can be seen for what they are: dislocating the familiar is the essence of this act, and—like his drama—Handke's poetry takes the mode of personal, direct address as most effective.

The slightest shift in language can be a key, and to make this point Handke again resorts to strategic (and sometimes startling) reversals. "What I am not . . . " is the short title of a "sentence biography," an apparently simple affair until the poet asks us to consider the different ways by which we linguistically characterize that state:

> What *I* am not:
> I am no voting bloc.
>
> What I UNFORTUNATELY am not:
> Unfortunately I am no hero
> Unfortunately I am no millionaire.
>
> What I am not THANK GOD:
> Thank God I am no automat
> Thank God I am not someone with whom you can do as you please.

And so forth. Positives demand the same qualifications that individual stanzas dictate: what I don't WANT, what I don't want BUT, what I DON'T want BUT ALSO don't want. Perspective as expressed in language can make the same subtle difference, as shown in "Changes during the Course of the Day":

> As soon as I step out on the street—a pedestrian steps out on the street.
> As soon as I enter the subway—a subway rider enters the subway.

These are indeed separations, but in certain acts the first person can become third person all at once, as in "I read the novel in the mass publication—and become one among millions," a posture we are certainly less aware of, even though these things happen all the time ("Then someone is recognized on a photo—and becomes an X"). In a similar manner, people identify themselves with objects, to the point (as was earlier demonstrated in *The Goalie's Anxiety at the Penalty Kick*) that they become those things themselves:

> MY invalids! says the nurse who works in the nursing home;
> MY kitchen! says the married woman;
> MY foreign minister! says the head of government;
> MY god! says someone who's startled.

At a certain point, Handke reminds us in "The Inverted World," act is exchanged with actor:

> I don't pronounce words, and words pronounce me;
> I go to the window and I am opened.

It is all a question of perception, which for Handke is just what poetry is (as drama is action and fiction is epistemology). "Abstractions of the Ball that Fell in the River" repeats the same scene ten times, varying perspective and the amount of subjective projection, until the activity is reduced to an equation in physics. One scene, or ten? It is all a matter of vision. "The Three Readings of the Law" are just that: the same passage read before an appreciative audience; a hostile one; and, finally, one that remains silent to the end. Cheering or heckling effectively changes the meanings of the words, although in isolation they remain the same. So, too, can context change meaning, as in either of these lines from "The Innerworld of the Outerworld of the Innerworld": "it is late afternoon as in a factual report about an assassination" or "as in the Western it is noon." In several poems Handke runs the same basic sentence (in terms of meaning) through several linguistic variations, much as at the start of *Kaspar*—are the sentences then the same, or different? Regardless of the reader's choice, he has been made aware of the parts of speech doing their different jobs in the variations. Above all, Handke wishes his readers to appreciate how various language can be, from a purity devoid of all communicative meaning ("The Japanese Hit Parade of May 25, 1968," which is simply listed) to phrases so packed with meaning that their words are contradictory ("Yes, the phrase 'as bright as day' means it is still night," p. 135).

If *The Innerworld of the Outerworld of the Innerworld* is made of instructions to the reader, *Nonsense and Happiness* (1974, translated 1976) is best characterized as a more contemplative book. "Life without Poetry" is its opening poem and a challenge that runs throughout the poems collected here. Without poetry, objects rule life; everything is completely expressionless, and in the title poem,

> even the prettiest sight now diminishes life.
> A bombing attack of nonsense on the world.

There would be no more dance to life, no action within it according to "Life Without Poetry":

> In the newspapers everything stood black on white
> and every phenomenon looked right from the start
> like a concept.

All becomes alien, and we cannot even act—only pretend to act:

> Everything pressed itself so much upon me
> that I lost my gift for fantasy
> Before the external magnificence of nature
> there was no imagining anything anymore
> and within the monotony of the sum total of daily impressions
> nothing particularly moved me.

But with a poetic perception—which for Handke is the realization of how language works within itself and as a system of correspondences between words and things—all is happily transformed:

> The shop was so bright and quiet
> the manager was counting the receipts
> and freezers hummed endearingly
> and the fact that the chives I bought
> were held together with a rubber band
> practically moved me to tears.

Life without poetry is death; with it, life becomes more than one can imagine. A traditional sentiment, of course, but it is one for which Handke has revolutionized poet–reader conventions in order to reaffirm.

VI. Peter Handke— Is the Goalie Exhausted?

> Because my fear of the nonsense is over
> they no longer need an order.
> And your own impression?—
> Because the nonsense is over the sight
> has simultaneously become the impression.
>
> —"Nonsense and Happiness"

As Peter Handke's literary career began twenty years ago, he seemed the perfect young rebel to overthrow the systematics of an exhausted literary modernism. In those tumultous days of "the death of the novel," the question was whether the great traditions of fiction could survive to do their work in the new intellectual and physical world so radically redescribed and redefined by postmodernism. In the early 1960s, Handke answered *no* and launched a career based on the orderly destruction of the system that underlie traditional fiction, drama, and poetry. His progress since then has been an index to the fate of postmodernism as a workable aesthetic.

Because of its characteristically deconstructive nature, the postmodernist project has been decried by many as a nihilistic affair. Among critics and theorists, Gerald Graff has led the attack on the absence of "an external standard of truth" in postmodern thought; without such standards of representation, Graff claims, "The weakness of much postmodern fiction lies in its inability or refusal to retain any moorings in social reality."[1] Among novelists, the late John Gardner has urged a revival of "moral fiction," arguing that "wherever possible moral art [should] hold up models of decent behavior; for example, characters in fiction, drama, and film whose basic goodness and struggle against confu-

1. Gerald Graff, *Literature Against Itself* (Chicago: University of Chicago Press, 1979), p. 209.

sion, error, and evil—in themselves and in others—give firm intellectual and emotional support to our own struggles."[2] At the root of Graff's and Gardner's objections is the fear that postmodern writing is antihumanistic and that in discarding humanism's standards of belief no humanly satisfactory art is possible.

Here is where the breadth of Handke's achievement is most helpfully apparent. Although his earliest works draw their energy from philosophical and aesthetic principles, his novels of the 1970s and 1980s can stand by themselves as valid artistic expressions drawing their energy from our age itself (and not simply its intellectual reflections). As the 1980s dawned, in fact, Peter Handke had become a leading figure in the establishment he had once struggled to overthrow. And, as always, the questions were many. Could postmodernism generate a literature as rich as the modernism it had striven to replace? What of the postmodernist's pertinence to readers: was there more here than a sterile self-reflexiveness, axiomatically correct but barren in terms of human interest and feeling? And especially in his step-by-step departures from the practice of drama, poetry, and even for a time fiction, did Peter Handke, the once explosive author of *The Goalie's Anxiety at the Penalty Kick,* find himself exhausted from the fray and ready for some time on the sidelines?

As Handke's success with the style of the New Sensibility proves, the answer to each of these questions is an emphatic *no!* Having reinvented fiction as an externally social artifact for our age, Handke without a moment's hesitation turned inward to a similar reinvention of his own most personal beliefs as a writer and as a human being. This sense of positive construction in both the external and internal spheres of his artistic life identify him as one of the preeminent writers of his generation, rather than as a servile practitioner of postmodernism's rebellious stage. Unlike the theorists of the French *nouveau roman,* who is systematically stripping away all anthropomorphic projections from the objects of this world (and hence producing a barrenly unhu-

2. John Gardner, *On Moral Fiction* (New York: Basic Books, 1978), p. 106.

man literature), Handke has focused his attention on just the opposite activity: on the sign-making practice itself, in which all human activities meet in social intercourse and in contact with the world. These signs, he reminds us, are not to be confused with actual things. But since those actual things can never be reliably known in themselves, why waste time with them? Humanism is just one system of arbitrary naming—isn't it far more human to be aware of how fraudulent any system is and to take joy instead in the unrestricted play of signs? In this activity, Handke argues, lies the greatest range of human interest.

With his sense of energy and exuberance Peter Handke is most like those innovative American fictionists—Donald Barthelme, Kurt Vonnegut, Ronald Sukenick, Richard Brautigan, and Steve Katz among them—who during these years transformed their country's writing into a renaissance of reinvention. Handke shares their positive sense of life, against those more experimentally remote writers (whether Alain Robbe-Grillet and Jean Ricardou in Europe or John Barth and Thomas Pynchon in America) who consider literature exhausted and therefore direct their efforts to the regressions of parody or labyrinthine interpretations of other interpretations. As the chief theorist of the innovative Americans, Ronald Sukenick has described this sense of affinity:

> My feeling is that you have always to move in the direction of the data of experience in "reality," whatever the chances that you can't do this. There's a line in Handke's *A Sorrow Beyond Dreams* where he talks about the effort to investigate and develop the psychology of a character—in this case, of his mom—and he says he realizes he can't do it, that he can never successfully arrive at the reality of that character. But at the same time he says that you have to try. I think that's true: you have to try, because it is only in making that effort to deal with those data that you finally create a legitimate fiction. In other words, you don't create a legitimate fiction merely by dealing with other fictions. One of the main purposes of really good writing is to destroy other really good writing, to destroy all the old concepts and formulas that come out of the best of the past. You should destroy them

> lovingly and with great consciousness and awareness of them, but always with the end in mind of getting beyond them. And knowing that they were also trying to do the same kind of thing.[3]

By attending to the unrestricted play of signs as signs, the writer gets hold not of reality itself but of man's construction of reality. "The artist becomes the inventor of experience from mere phenomena," Sukenick explains. "That is, we're confronted with phenomena and we want experience. Experience is phenomena taken in and made relevant to the individual psyche."[4]

It is Handke's richness of response within this program that makes his work so valuable. He can still tell stories, but makes them more humanly interesting by bringing attention to their sign-making activity. He also knows that there are other structural devices besides narrative—devices more elementally close to human experience, such as the rhythms of rock music that provide patterns for *Offending the Audience* and the see-saw nature of existence that characterizes *Self-Accusation*. His four most recent books within the style of the New Sensibility stand as the confident realization of a literary program two decades in the making. Since 1963, Handke's work has addressed the problems of literature within the new postmodern aesthetic: first the outmoded conventions and expectations that needed to be banished; then an attempt to dramatize these struggles in human terms (leading to candidly personal applications); and, finally, the fully complex novels that not only tested the principles of postmodernism in intimately human terms but also established a positive program for the author himself. As content became effaced from literary works, processes of composition have assumed increasing importance, and Handke's achievement has been to find a way to make them as humanly interesting and fictionally dramatic as any

3. Larry McCaffery, interview with Ronald Sukenick, in *Anything Can Happen: Interviews with Contemporary American Novelists*, ed. Tom LeClair and Larry McCaffery (Urbana: University of Illinois Press, 1983), p. 282.

4. Charlotte M. Meyer, "An Interview with Ronald Sukenick," *Contemporary Literature* 23 (Spring 1982): 135.

stories of the Great Tradition. His earliest work in all genres, from the stories of *Greeting the Board of Directors* and the novelistic experiments of *The Hornets* and *The Peddler,* through the dramatic deconstructions of *Offending the Audience* and the parallel poetic exercises of *The Innerworld of the Outerworld of the Innerworld,* are both the clearing of tradition from his own desk and instructive disciplines for those who wish to learn how to read the new postmodern literature. By 1970, as Western culture was catching up with this aesthetic, Handke was able to say goodbye for a time to drama in favor of poems and novels that could dramatize the societal and political process now so evident in the streets. It is therefore inevitable, with these artistic and social bases firmly established, that Handke would proceed toward more complexly intimate situations for both his characters (as in *A Moment of True Feeling* and *The Left-Handed Woman*) and himself (notably *The Lesson of Sainte Victoire* and *Children's Story*). Is the goalie exhausted? *Satisfied* would be a more appropriate description, particularly in view of recent turns in his career. Along with continuing his own writing, Handke has been using his linguistic talents and considerable reputation to bring attention to literary works in other languages, translating from the French and Slovenian and preparing a German edition of Walker Percy's *Moviegoer* as well.

Peter Handke's progress has been from the negative to the positive, from the linguistically problematic to the confident reassumption of purpose for art, from the externally austere to the richly personal. In the process, he has found a way to address the human condition within the new aesthetic terms of our age and to calm the fears of readers who suspected that the loss of literature's greatest traditions would jeapordize all human interest as well. The lesson of postmodernism has been that the abstraction of content is not a loss; rather, it leads directly to the most essential element of human concern—now experienced with the full force of readerly and writerly attention, because the distracting and diluting conventions of an earlier age can no longer interfere with the business of making literary art. To have become the grand old man of literature at the relatively young age of forty would be, for Peter Handke, more of an inevitability than an innovation, given the centrality of his work to the essence of what literary art must be.

Books by Peter Handke

Fiction

Die Hornissen (The Hornets). Frankfurt: Suhrkamp, 1966.

Der Hausierer (The Peddler). Frankfurt: Suhrkamp, 1967.

Begrüssung des Aufsichstrats (Greeting the Board of Directors). Salzburg: Residenz, 1967. Collected in *Prosa Gedichte Theaterstücke Hörspiel Aufsätze* (Frankfurt: Suhrkamp, 1969), pp. 9–108, from which we have quoted.

Die Angst des Tormanns beim Elfmeter (The Goalie's Anxiety at the Penalty Kick). Frankfurt: Suhrkamp, 1970. Translated by Michael Roloff. New York: Farrar, Straus & Giroux, 1972. London: Methuen, 1977.

Der Kurze Brief zum lagen Abschied (Short Letter, Long Farewell). Frankfurt: Suhrkamp, 1972. Translated by Ralph Manheim. New York: Farrar, Straus & Giroux, 1974. London: Methuen, 1977.

Wünschloses Unglück (A Sorrow Beyond Dreams). Salzburg: Residenz, 1972. Translated by Ralph Manheim. New York: Farrar, Straus & Giroux, 1975. London: Condor Books, Souvenir Press, 1976.

Die Stunde der wahren Emfindung (A Moment of True Feeling). Frankfurt: Suhrkamp, 1975. Translated by Ralph Manheim. New York: Farrar, Straus & Giroux, 1977.

Die linkshändige Frau (The Left-Handed Woman). Frankfurt: Suhrkamp, 1976. Translated by Ralph Manheim. New York: Farrar, Straus & Giroux, 1978. London: Methuen, 1980.

Das Gewicht der Welt (The Weight of the World). Salzburg: Residenz, 1977.

Langsame Heimkehr (Slow Journey Home). Frankfurt: Suhrkamp, 1979.

Die Lehre der Sainte Victoire (The Lesson of Sainte Victoire). Frankfurt: Suhrkamp, 1980.

Kindergeschichte (Children's Story). Frankfurt: Sukrkamp, 1981.

Drama

Publikumsbeschimpfung und andere Sprechstücke (also includes *Self-Accusation* and *Prophecy*). Frankfurt: Suhrkamp, 1966.

Quodlibet. Frankfurt: Verlag der Autoren, 1970.

Stücke 1 (includes *Offending the Audience, Prophecy, Self-Accusation, Calling for Help,* and *Kaspar*). Frankfurt: Suhrkamp, 1972.

Stücke 2 (includes *My Foot My Tutor, Quodlibet,* and *The Ride Across Lake Constance*). Frankfurt: Suhrkamp, 1973.

Kasper and Other Plays (also includes *Offending the Audience* and *Self-Accusation*). Translated by Michael Roloff. New York: Farrar, Straus & Giroux, 1969.

Offending the Audience and Self-Accusation. Translated by Michael Roloff. London: Methuen, 1971.

Kaspar. Translated by Michael Roloff. London: Methuen, 1972.

The Ride Across Lake Constance and Other Plays (also includes *Prophecy, Calling for Help, My Foot My Tutor, Quodlibet,* and *They Are Dying Out*). Translated by Michael Roloff. New York: Farrar, Straus & Giroux, 1977.

Über die Dörfer (Beyond the Villages). Frankfurt: Suhrkamp, 1981.

Poetry

Deutsche Gedichte. Frankfurt: Euphorion, 1969.

Die Innerwelt der Aussenwelt der Innerwelt (The Innerworld of the Outerworld of the Innerworld). Frankfurt: Suhrkamp, 1969. Selected poems translated by Michael Roloff. New York: Seabury Press, 1974.

Als das Wünschen noch geholfen hat. Frankfurt: Suhrkamp, 1974.

Das Ende des Flanierens (translated as *Nonsense and Happiness*). Vienna: Davidpress, 1976. Translated by Michael Roloff. New York: Urizen Books, 1976.

Essays

Ich bein ein Bewohner des Elfenbeinturms (I Am an Ivory Tower Dweller). Frankfurt: Suhrkamp, 1972.